PROCLAIMING THE GOOD NEWS: HOMILIES FOR THE 'B' CYCLE

by John Jay Hughes

WITH A FOREWORD BY
JOSEPH CARDINAL BERNARDIN

OUR SUNDAY VISITOR, INC.
HUNTINGTON, INDIANA 46750

ACKNOWLEDGMENTS

Besides those works cited throughout this book, the author is grateful for the use of scriptural quotations gleaned from various sources, including those taken from the *New American Bible*, © 1970, Confraternity of Christian Doctrine. All rights reserved.

Imprimatur:
Most Rev. Edward J. O'Donnell
Auxiliary Bishop and Vicar General
Archdiocese of St. Louis
June 13, 1984

Library of Congress Catalog Card No.: 84-60750
International Standard Book No.: 0-87973-723-9

Published, printed, and bound in the U.S.A. by
Our Sunday Visitor, Inc.
200 Noll Plaza
Huntington, Indiana 46750

723

*In gratitude
to those who first awakened in me
a hunger for God's word,
and impressed me with its power . . .*

*William Thomas Manning
Alan Griffith Whittemore, O.H.C.
Bernard Iddings Bell*

Table of Contents

Foreword

Since the Second Vatican Council, we have tended to focus on the Gospel message in a new way. It has become the heart and the focus of our Christian life and ministry. We find ourselves measuring our positions and our behavior in terms of the Scriptures. Preaching and teaching the Word is simply essential to Christian ministry.

To be effective teachers of the Gospel, we must first listen attentively to the Word ourselves. This clearly implies both study and prayerful reflection. St. Jerome said it very succinctly: "Ignorance of the Scriptures is ignorance of Christ." Encounter with the biblical text provides not only guidance and nourishment but also challenge to the way we live our lives.

It is not easy for us to accept the fullness of the message we find in the Gospel or to incorporate it into our daily lives. But that is what we are called to do. God speaks his Word to us. After we have listened attentively, we are expected to respond willingly and wholeheartedly. This means ongoing conversion on our part as Christian ministers — before, after, and during our ministry of proclamation and preaching.

About seven years ago, I came to understand that the pace of my life and the direction of my activity were unfocused, uncentered in a significant way. This created a certain unrest. I came to realize that I needed to make some changes in my life, and chief among these was a renewal of personal prayer.

Mention of prayer may evoke an image of "saying" prayers, of reciting formulas. I mean something quite different. When we speak of the renewal of prayer in our lives, we are speaking of reconnecting ourselves with the larger mystery of life and of our common existence. This implies becoming disciplined in the use of our time, in the use of centering prayer, and in the development of a contemplative stance toward life.

When this happens, we begin to experience healing, integration, wholeness, peacefulness. We begin to hear more clearly the echoes of the Word in our own lives, in our own hearts. And as that Word takes root in the depths of our being, it begins to grow and to transform the way we live. It affects our relationships with people around us and above all our relationship with the Lord. From this rootedness flow our energies, our ministry, our ways of loving. From this core we can proclaim the Lord Jesus and his Gospel not only with faith and conviction but also with love and compassion.

The people of God need and deserve effective proclamation of God's Word and good homilies. A disciplined approach to prepare for these ministries can meet these needs and move people more deeply into a community of faith with one another and ultimately into the very heart of God.

This book by John Jay Hughes is an important resource for helping us understand the Word of God and its deeper implications for our lives. We owe him a debt of gratitude.

Joseph Cardinal Bernardin
ARCHBISHOP OF CHICAGO

Introduction

In a widely noted address concluding his presidency of the National Conference of Catholic Bishops in November 1977, Joseph L. Bernardin, then Archbishop of Cincinnati, expressed concern about the large number of Catholics "who have never experienced true conversion, whose understanding of what the Catholic Faith really means and the demands it makes of its adherents is minimal." Echoing a fundamental theme of the Second Vatican Council, he affirmed: "The most important task of a bishop is to proclaim Christ Jesus and his Good News in such a way as to elicit a deep, personal commitment to him and acceptance of his message."

The American Lutheran Wallace E. Fisher strongly supports these views:

> Millions of mainline Protestant and Roman Catholic lay people have never made a clear-headed, gallant commitment to Christ, because they have not heard him preached intelligibly. . . . The revival of the church in the West waits for a powerful, widespread revival of biblical preaching in the Protestant, Roman Catholic, and Orthodox churches in the closing decades of the twentieth century.
>
> (Wallace E. Fisher,
> *Who Dares to Preach? The Challenge of Biblical Preaching*)

What are the obstacles to such preaching? I should like to discuss three: neglect of Scripture, neglect of theology, and neglect of personal prayer.

Neglect of Scripture

Less than a quarter century has passed since Catholics were taught that missing the Liturgy of the Word on a Sunday or other day of obligation was "only a venial sin" that need not be confessed. The "important" part of the Mass, ac-

11

cording to this teaching, was the repetition, by a duly ordained priest, of Jesus' words over the bread and wine at the Last Supper. This was what made Catholic worship something utterly different from a Protestant service of "mere" Bible-reading and preaching — and vastly superior. The Liturgy of the Word, we were told in those not-so-distant days, was an "unimportant" embellishment of the "essential" part of the Mass: consecration and Communion. (See Heribert Jone, *Moral Theology* [Westminster, Maryland, 1960] No. 195.)

Vatican II recovered an essential element of Catholic faith which for more than four centuries had been submerged beneath anti-Protestant polemic: respect for Scripture. "The church has always venerated the divine scriptures just as she venerates the body of the Lord," the Council Fathers declared in the *Constitution on Divine Revelation* (21).

Is that really true? Well (to use a phrase beloved of the old Latin manuals), *secundum quid* — in a sense. In theory we have always venerated Scripture in the way the Council claimed. In practice, however, we have too often failed to do so. The teaching just cited about the "important" and "unimportant" parts of the Mass is an example of this failure. Unfortunately, it was by no means unique.

The Council reinforced its teaching about the importance of Scripture by its own example. Each day's session began, after the celebration of the Mass, with the enthronement in the midst of the assembly not of the monstrance with the consecrated host (as might have been expected, given the emphasis of Catholic spirituality and teaching since the Reformation), but of the written word of God. The Council could hardly have given a more striking visible expression of its teaching that the Church's "teaching office is not above the word of God, but serves it, teaching only what has been handed on, listening to it devoutly, guarding it scrupulously and explaining it faithfully in accord with a divine commission and with the help of the Holy Spirit; it draws from this one

12

deposit of faith everything which it presents for belief as divinely revealed" (*Revelation*, 10).

It would not be reasonable to expect that the Council's teaching would be fully incorporated in Church life in the short space of two decades. Cardinal Hume of Westminster has said that we shall still be assimilating the Council's teaching at the end of the century. Though the rediscovery of Scripture has already influenced Catholic life profoundly, lack of reverence for Scripture is still with us. All too often lectors (including the clergy) fail to become familiar with the readings before Mass and hence read them in a perfunctory and slipshod manner.

A more serious form of scriptural neglect is failure to base preaching upon serious study of the biblical text, with the help of good commentaries. A newspaper article in my files reports that the August 1980 convention of the National Office of Black Catholics suggested that "the spiritual and intellectual quality of sermons could be enhanced by allowing more lay persons and deacons to give the homily." What a commentary on the homiletic efforts of us who are supposed to have been professionally trained in Scripture — to suggest that those without such training could be better guides to understanding the word of God than we are.

No one could realistically demand, or even desire, that today's increasingly overworked parish clergy become mini-Scripture scholars. Yet in a day in which we priests have strong competition from lay people in such areas as counseling and social action (to name two activities that take much of our time), might we not reexamine the time we give to an area in which we have virtually no competition: becoming professionally competent ministers of God's word?

Neglect of Theology

Here the situation is the reverse of the one we have just been discussing. Our neglect of Scripture since the Reformation produced a deficit that we are still laboring to overcome.

In theology the record prior to Vatican II was one of emphasis so strong that it has produced among many Catholics today almost a revulsion against doctrine and theology.

The manuals of theology used in almost all Catholic seminaries until Vatican II tried to present the whole of theology in the form of propositions to be learned by heart. The objections to each of these propositions were set forth — and refuted from Scripture and Tradition. Students inevitably gained the impression that if they studied this impressive body of material diligently, they would have, by the time of ordination, a thorough working knowledge of the whole of the Church's teaching. From the point of view of Church authority, priests so trained would be "safe" in the pulpit and in the confessional.

Since Vatican II we have become keenly aware that, however true the propositions contained in the manuals might have been, they too often addressed questions of little interest to the people in the pews. Out of embarrassment at having been blind to this situation for so long, not a few Catholics have embraced the old liberal Protestant idea that "what people need is not doctrine, but love." (This may have been a factor in the contention of the Black Catholics' convention, cited above, that preaching could be made more fruitful by the participation of those without formal theological training.)

A compound of the two Greek words *theos* (God) and *logos* (word), theology is quite simply "God-talk" or "talk about God." It is as true today as it was twenty centuries ago that "man does not live on bread alone but on every word that comes from the mouth of God" (Matthew 4:4, citing Deuteronomy 8:3). People today are weary not of theology but of bad and irrelevant theology. As we approach the end of this bloodiest and most chaotic of all centuries in recorded history, people are searching with a hunger that beggars description for a "word of the Lord" that will enable them to make sense of life, and to face death with courage and the assurance that it is something more than the snuffing out of a candle.

14

The primary source of this "word of the Lord" is holy Scripture. Catholics have always known, however (even if today, for the reasons just outlined, some of us seem to forget), that the inspired words of Scripture cannot be fruitfully applied to contemporary situations without interpretation. For this we need theology.

Theology tries to set forth the unchanging content of the Church's faith (the dogmas) in language that is intelligible and relevant to people in each successive generation. Hence theology's task, as has been often said, is never finished — for two reasons. First, because language, people, and the world are constantly changing; and second, because all language, being human and finite, is inadequate to express fully the truth about God and his world; for that truth is both divine and infinite.

Hence those who are commissioned as ministers of God's word and sacraments need to be constantly perfecting their theological skills. Few of us are called to be professional theologians, just as few are called to be professional exegetes. All of us, however, need to develop and maintain a practical working knowledge of Scripture, and of the Church's doctrinal tradition, that is at least equal to the expertise expected of other professionals in our society.

To think that we can adequately serve the people of God with the knowledge acquired years ago in seminary (whether before Vatican II or since), and on the strength of zeal, a warm heart, and a pleasant smile, is an affront to our calling. Such an approach to ministry is as irresponsible as that of the aspiring physician who thinks he can serve his patients with compassion and a good bedside manner, but without the grinding work involved in mastering pathology, anatomy, clinical practice, and the other medical skills. It could also be compared to the attitude of the law student who supposes that passion for justice can substitute for acquisition of the lawyer's stock-in-trade: contracts, torts, criminal law, taxation, bankruptcy, and the rest.

15

Neglect of Prayer

The new liturgy, as has been often noted, makes heavier demands than the old on liturgist and worshipers alike. Of the latter the new liturgy demands "active participation." In the clericalized and mostly silent liturgy of the past, the participation of many worshipers was largely passive — which is not to say that it was not genuine and spiritually fruitful.

The demands on the present-day liturgist are heavier still. Facing the people, and speaking aloud in their own language, he is subject to far closer scrutiny than was formerly the case when the congregation gazed mostly at his back, heard little of what he said, and understood less. Spiritually sensitive worshipers have always been able to discern whether the celebrant was a man of God. Now only the most insensitive fail to distinguish between the priest who stands at the altar and in the pulpit like Moses, "seeing him who is invisible" (Hebrews 11:27), and the functionary who pays the Lord lip-service while his heart is far away (see Matthew 15:8).

The crucial difference is in the way we "know" the Lord whom we address in prayer, and of whom we speak in the homily. Do we know all *about* him? Or do we know him as we know a dearly loved friend? The answer to these questions is determined outside the worshipers' view: in the "secret place" of private prayer recommended by Jesus (Matthew 6:6).
Mount (Matthew 6:6).

Jesus spoke in that passage from his own lived experience. Even the most casual reader of the Gospels cannot fail to notice the time Jesus spent in solitary, private prayer. In those hours alone with his heavenly Father Jesus gained the spiritual power that enabled him to say to rough workingmen, "Come, follow me" — and have them obey him on the spot. It was in prayer that Jesus became the preacher of whom Mark wrote: "And they were astonished at his teaching, for he taught them with authority and not like the scribes" (1:22). If Jesus, whose interior resources were greater by far than ours, needed those times alone with God, we are fools and guilty fools if we neglect prayer.

16

If we want to speak with an authority like his (and which of us does not?), we must spend time alone with God, waiting upon him in silence, day in and day out, week after week, month after month, year after year — even when, indeed *especially* when, God seems to answer only with silence.

Our goal should be preaching that causes our hearers to say with Cleopas and his companion: "Did we not feel our hearts on fire as he talked with us . . . and explained the scriptures to us?" (Luke 24:32). We *can* preach like that — but only on the condition that *our* hearts have first been touched by the divine fire. For that we must spend time alone with God. There is no other way.

* * *

No one who neglects Scripture, theology, or prayer can preach effectively, let alone with spiritual power. If there is evidence that these things are neglected by preachers today, there is also abundant contrary evidence. It would be difficult to find any period in Church history when the interest of Catholics in Scripture was as strong as it is today. Neglect of theology is so foreign to our whole Catholic tradition that it cannot make lasting inroads, even if the consequences of this neglect promise to be with us for a considerable time. Finally, the evidence of a hunger for prayer among today's Catholics, clergy and laypeople alike, is too well known to require summary here.

The interest in preaching is palpable. No publisher would be willing otherwise to publish a book such as this. Especially hopeful is the fine study commissioned by the U.S. Bishops' Committee on Priestly Life and Ministry, *Fulfilled in your Hearing: The Homily in the Sunday Assembly* (Washington, D.C., 1982).

Every recent public opinion survey documents the hunger of Catholics for good preaching. Father Walter J. Burghardt, S.J., whose authority on such matters is beyond question, has written:

17

In thirty-six years of priestly preaching, not once have I encountered an unresponsive congregation, not once a believing community that could not be stirred.

(Walter J. Burghardt, Tell the Next Generation:
Homilies and Near Homilies [New York, 1980], p. 16)

A sign of special hope today is the example of Pope John Paul II. Can his magnetic attraction be explained simply in terms of showmanship and a personality cult? What is it that causes hundreds of thousands of people in country after country to journey long distances, to stand for hours in blazing heat, or in cold and rain, to see and to hear a man whose words reach them mostly in a heavily accented version of their own language, and whose message large numbers of them accept only in part?

We cannot answer these questions unless we realize that this pope presents himself to people primarily as *a preacher*. His preaching is effective because it is rooted in Scripture; because it reflects a total theological view; and because it comes from a man whom people the world over, whether believers or not, perceive to be a man of faith and a man of prayer.

What further encouragement do we need to "go and do the same"? (Luke 10:37).

John Jay Hughes

ST. LOUIS, MISSOURI
CONVERSION OF ST. PAUL, 1984

18

First Sunday in Advent

Isaiah 63:16-17,19; 64:2-7; 1 Corinthians 1:3-9; Mark 13:33-37

"OH, THAT YOU WOULD REND THE HEAVENS..."

- *To proclaim the Advent message of hope in a time of disillusion and discouragement.*

How many people here today can remember the mood of Catholics twenty-three years ago, on the first Sunday in Advent 1961? Pope John XXIII had summoned the Second Vatican Council three years before. In less than a year it would begin. It was a time of excitement and hope. The Holy Father said the Council would be a new pentecost. Many people thought it might bring the reunion of separated Christians.

Today, almost two decades after the Council's close, how many of those high hopes have been fulfilled? Not many. There has been no new pentecost, and no Christian reunion. Our churches are not fuller today, but emptier. In place of the unified, self-confident Church that today's middle-aged and older Catholics remember from their youth, we have turmoil, disarray, and confusion. For all too many Catholics today the dominant mood is one of disillusion and discouragement.

For this mood the Church gives us on this first Sunday in Advent a "word of the Lord." We find it in today's first reading: a passage addressed by the prophet to God's people after their return from exile in Babylon. They had come back to Jerusalem with high hopes — every bit as high as the hopes Catholics had on the eve of the Council twenty-three years ago. Now, years later, the people's hopes remained unfulfilled. The temple, far from being restored, was still in

19

ruins (see Isaiah 64:10f). The nation's life had not been renewed. People were still trapped in the self-centeredness of
sin. God seemed to have abandoned them. How well the
prophet's words describe their desolate state:

> We have all withered like leaves, and our guilt carries us away
> like the wind. There is none who calls upon your name, who
> rouses himself to cling to you; for you have hidden your face
> from us and have delivered us up to our guilt.

In the midst of this desolation the prophet prays for a dramatic intervention from on high, which would prove that God
had not deserted his people. "Oh, that you would rend the
heavens and come down!" How many of us could pray that
same prayer today!

Even as he utters the words, however, the prophet reaf-
firms his faith that God has *not* deserted his people, despite
all appearances to the contrary.

> Yet, O Lord, you are our father; we are the clay and you are the
> potter; we are all the work of your hands.

Through weariness, discouragement, disillusion — in the
Church, and in our own personal lives — God is *shaping* us according to his plan, as the potter shapes the lump of clay on
his swiftly turning wheel; kneading it, coaxing it, forming it
into something beautiful, and then fixing its perfect sym-
metry forever in the intense heat of his furnace. The things
that weigh us down are signs *not* of God's absence, but of his
presence. He is not finished with us yet. He is still working on
us.

Our part in this work of formation is to be faithful, to
watch and wait. "Be constantly on the watch! Stay awake!"

Jesus tells us in the Gospel. The prophet's message is the same:

> No ear has ever heard, no eye ever seen, any God but you doing such deeds *for those who wait for him.* Would that you might meet us doing right, that we were mindful of you in our ways!

There is the word of the Lord for us today.

"Oh, that you would rend the heavens and come down!" It is the church's fundamental faith and special Advent message that this prayer has been answered *already*! The gospel writer Mark was convinced of this when he wrote of Jesus' baptism: "No sooner had Jesus come up out of the water than he saw the heavens *torn apart* and the Spirit, like a dove, descending on him" (1:10, Jerusalem Bible).

Every Mass is a rending of the heavens. Jesus comes to be with us to give us medicine for the wounds we have received in the battle of life, food to strengthen us for the journey still ahead. What prayer could be more fitting for us at this Mass than Isaiah's words from our first reading: "Would that you might meet us doing right, that we were mindful of you in our ways!"

That is the important thing. Don't bother so much about "avoiding evil." Concentrate instead on doing right, on being mindful of the Lord in all your ways. Then, whenever the Lord comes, he will find you ready. Then, you will know that Paul's beautiful words from our second reading are *true*:

> He will strengthen you to the end, so that you will be blameless on the day of our Lord Jesus Christ. God is faithful, and it was he who called you to fellowship with his Son, Jesus Christ the Lord.

Second Sunday in Advent

Mark 1:1-8

"PREPARE A WAY FOR THE LORD."

• *To help the hearers repent, and to show the Spirit's role in repentance.*

John was clothed in camel's hair, and wore a leather belt around his waist. His food was grasshoppers and wild honey.

If John lived today, we would call him a dropout, a hippie, and a food nut. Can someone as bizarre as that have anything to say to us at the end of the twentieth century?

John's message had two parts. He proclaimed:
• repentance and baptism for the forgiveness of sins; and —
• the coming of one mightier than himself who would baptize not with water, but with the Holy Spirit of the living God.

In placing this twofold message before us today, the Church is saying that it *is* relevant — and important. Let's see why.

Repentance means "turning around," a total reversal of the whole direction of my life. All of us come into this world turned in on ourselves. What *we* want *right now* is what we must have at any price. Dr. Spock, the well-known baby doctor, tells a story that illustrates this. In his practice he saw a three-month-old infant that was as good as gold as long as it was held and caressed by its mother. The moment the baby was put down to sleep, however, it screamed its little lungs out. Babies and small children cannot do anything about this inborn self-centeredness. They cannot even hide it.

Part of growing to maturity is learning to overcome our selfishness. The first step is admitting that it is there: that we

22

are not the people we want to be and ought to be; that we fall short of what *God* wanted us to be when, through our parents, he gave us the precious gift of life.

The people who came to John to be baptized in the Jordan River were making that fundamental admission. They were facing up to the brokenness of their lives; admitting that their lives were a tangle of loose ends and shattered resolutions. That is the first step in repentance: admitting that we fall short, that our lives are disordered and unmanageable.

Many people get that far. But they think it is up to *them* to mend their brokenness. By trying harder they think they can "clean up their act" and "get it all together," as we often say today. The *second* part of John's message demolishes all optimistic ideas about repairing our disordered lives through greater willpower and self-discipline.

> One more powerful than I is to come after me.... I have baptized you in water; he will baptize you in the Holy Spirit.

John was telling people that admitting their self-centeredness and the disorder of their lives was only the first step. They need to admit that their disordered lives could be put right only by a power *greater* than their own, a power from *outside*. This is the power of God's Holy Spirit.

Are you completely satisfied with *your* life? If you knew you were to die tonight, is there nothing you would seriously regret or want changed? If so, then there is little point in your being here. Then the Gospel of Jesus Christ is not for you. For this Gospel is good news: the good news that God loves people who are *not* satisfied with their lives; who are weighed down with the consciousness of all the things they would like to have done differently if they knew they were to die tonight.

23

Only for people like that does John's Advent message of repentance make any sense at all.

And for such people the *second* half of John's message is as important as the first. The changes that need to take place in our lives will not occur without our best effort — true. But our best effort alone is insufficient. Thinking *we* must first get our act together before God will love and bless us leads either to pride or to despair. Either we persuade ourselves that we *have* got our act together, and now it is up to God to reward us for our services rendered — which is pride. *Or* we get so discouraged at constantly falling short that we fall into despair.

The Gospel message of God's freely given love is for those who know that their act needs to be cleaned up; who have tried to clean it up and failed; and who recognize that there is One and One alone who can do *for* them what they could never do for themselves: make straight in the wasteland of their lives a highway for himself.

If you recognize the need for the healing, cleansing touch of God's Holy Spirit; if you are ready to abandon your efforts to get your life in order by your own will-power and good resolutions; if you recognize that even your best efforts will be fruitless until you turn your life over to God — then, and *only* then, are you ready for the coming at Christmas of God's Son: your savior and redeemer — but also your brother, and your best friend.

Third Sunday in Advent

Isaiah 61:1-2, 10-11; 1 Thessalonians 5:16-24; John 1:6-8, 19-28

"MY SOUL REJOICES IN GOD."

- *To help the hearers experience Christian joy.*

One of the beauties of childhood is the ability of little children to rejoice at the coming of Christmas. Many of us here today know a young child who is in a fever of excitement, wondering what presents will appear under the tree on Christmas morning. Through children we recall the joy *we* once felt in childhood at the approach of Christmas.

Joy is the theme of today's liturgy. The first reading and the Gospel contain the joyful proclamation that the long-promised servant of God is at hand: his anointed one, the Messiah. "My soul rejoices in God," we responded in the responsorial psalm, which was Mary's hymn of joy at the coming birth of her son. And in the second reading Paul tells us to "rejoice always."

Can we rejoice always? Certainly not in the sense of making life one long celebration. Every life contains sadness and hurt. More than one person here today is asking: "What reason do *I* have for joy?"

If that is *your* question, then let me speak very personally to you. No matter what hurt you bring here — loneliness, disappointment, bereavement, or the pain of bitter injustice — you have, along *with* the hurt and the tears, *every reason for joy.*

Let me tell you about three. Each one is closely associated with Jesus Christ. We can rejoice because:

25

Jesus is behind us;
Jesus is with us; and
Jesus is ahead of us.

Jesus Is Behind Us

At the first Christmas Jesus entered into our human life, sharing everything that life brings us, sin excepted. Jesus experienced life's joys (think of the wedding at Cana), but also its deepest sorrows (recall how he wept at the death of his friend Lazarus: John 11:35). On the cross Jesus experienced the most monstrous injustice and the most agonizing suffering. The babe in the crib at Bethlehem and the man on the cross at Calvary both proclaim: God cares. God loves you. Life is *not* meaningless, provided it is lived for *him*, in the strength that he alone can give. Sensing all this in advance, Mary rejoiced in the words we repeated a moment ago: "My soul rejoices in my God." Despite suffering, injustice, and pain, we rejoice because Jesus has shared it all. Jesus is behind us. We have a further reason to rejoice, however, because —

Jesus Is With Us

He is never distant, even when we are far from him. To be with Jesus, all that is necessary is a simple inward movement of the heart. Short prayers are often the best: "Jesus, help me" — "My Lord and my God" — or simply the holy names, repeated as we cross the street, drive down the highway, or stand in the checkout line at the supermarket: "Jesus, Mary, Joseph."

Jesus is with us too in his holy word: proclaimed here in the assembly of God's people, or read over quietly by ourselves. More than one person here has experienced, through hearing or reading holy Scripture, what Jesus' two friends felt that first Easter day on the road to Emmaus: "Did not our hearts burn within us as he . . . explained the scriptures to us?" (Luke 24:32). Jesus is with us in the sacraments, especially in the sacrament we are celebrating now: the Holy Eucharist. Jesus is with us also (though we too often forget this) whenever we encounter someone in any kind of need. One day we shall hear him saying to us: "Inasmuch as you have done it — or failed to do it — to one of these least brothers or sisters, you have done it — or failed to do it — to me" (see Matthew 25:40, 45).

So we rejoice because Jesus has entered into human life and is behind us. We rejoice also because Jesus is always with us. Our final reason for joy is the knowledge that —

Jesus Is Ahead of Us

The one future event that is absolutely certain is death. If death were simply the snuffing out of a candle, we should have little reason for joy. But death is infinitely more. Death is the great transformation, the passage from this life, limited in a hundred ways and shadowed by suffering, to life eternal: where there will be no limitations, no suffering, where God will wipe away all tears from our eyes. We are saddened by the certainty of dying, and by the parting from loved ones that death entails. At the same time, we can rejoice to know that when we come to walk that last stretch of life's way, we shall not be alone. Jesus will be with us. He will welcome us at the end to the eternal dwelling place that he has gone ahead to prepare for us (see John 14:2).

Do we have reason for joy? Certainly, we have *every* reason for joy! We rejoice to know that Jesus is behind us: he has entered into our human life and shared it to the full. We rejoice

27

because Jesus is always with us: never distant, even when we stray far from him. We rejoice because Jesus is ahead of us: the great encounter with him who loves us beyond our imagining is coming daily and hourly closer.

And so I, his unworthy but joyful servant, invite you to join now in the great feast in which we celebrate this joy; where we encounter, as intimately as we can in this life, "Jesus Christ, the same yesterday, today, yes and forever" (Hebrews 13:8).

Fourth Sunday in Advent

2 Samuel 7:1-5, 8-11, 16; Romans 16:25-27; Luke 1:26-38

MARY, THE WOMAN OF FAITH.

- *To show how Mary is the model of trusting faith.*

We all need heroes: people we can look up to and admire. Heroes give us hope when we are discouraged. They convince us that life is worth living. Perhaps the greatest hero of Jesus' people was King David. His career was as romantic as that of any film star or athlete today. From a lowly shepherd boy David had risen to be king of God's chosen people. On the way David had many setbacks, hard struggles against determined enemies, and at least one fall into serious sin.

Todays' first reading told of David's desire to build a temple worthy of God. The prophet Nathan approved David's proposal — until he learned that *God* had other plans. David would not build a house for God. God would build a house for him — not a structure of wood and stone, but a family or dynasty. After David's death, however, God's plan seemed to collapse. The nation over which David had ruled was defeated and carried off into exile. The royal "house" that God had established for David seemed to have come to an end.

In the second reading, however, Paul said that God *had* kept his promise to David. He did so through his Son, Jesus. Jesus is the "missing link" who supplies the explanation of what till then had been hidden. Paul calls Jesus "the mystery hidden for many ages, but now manifested . . . and at the command of the eternal God made known to all the nations."

On this fourth Sunday in Advent, however, it is not Jesus

whom the Church places before us in the Gospel, but his mother Mary. How much we Catholics used to hear about Mary. How little we seem to hear about her today. Yet Mary has a special message for us today: a message of *faith*.

Faith used to be for us Catholics "*the* faith": the articles of belief contained in the creed, which we hold to be true on the authority of the Church which teaches them to us. Not one of those truths has been altered or repealed. Every one of them remains important. There is an even more important meaning of faith, however — a *personal* meaning. Faith is not merely mental acceptance of truths. It is *trust in a person*. The creed that contains the truths of faith begins not, "We believe *that* . . ." but "We believe *in* . . ." The one we believe in, whom we trust, is God.

We learn the meaning of the *truths* of faith from catechisms and similar works. We learn faith in the sense of *personal trust* not from books, but from people. The greatest model for faith in this fundamental and personal sense is the woman the Church places before us in today's Gospel: Mary, the trusting and faith-filled mother of the Lord.

The kind of trusting faith we see in Mary reckons with the possibility that even our best and holiest ideas of God may be inadequate; that they must be broken and rebuilt anew. Mary displays a faith that is prepared for darkness and trial, yet is always open to God. Hers is a faith that threw her totally upon God, permitting him to do with her and her life whatever he would.

Yet Mary's faith was very modern. It was not a blind faith. Mary doubted and questioned. "How can this be?" she asked the angel who told her she was to be the mother of God's Son. What Mary questioned, however, was not so much God, as her own ability to *understand* God and his plan for her life. Yet even in the midst of perplexity, Mary confessed that God knew best, even if she could not understand what he was about: "Let it be done to me as you say," she told the angel.

Mary's assent had to be constantly renewed, through many sufferings. Upon discovering that she was expecting a child before their marriage, Joseph wanted to break their engagement (Matthew 1:19). Later Simeon prophesied that Mary's Son would be "a sign which men reject," and that Mary too would be "pierced to the heart" (Luke 2:35). The only story we have of Jesus' childhood shows him to have been uncomfortably independent (Luke 2:41-52).

After reaching manhood Jesus left his mother, as he demanded that his followers should leave their parents. He said that his true mother and relatives were not those related by blood, but those who did his will (Luke 8:21). Sometimes, as at the wedding in Cana, Jesus seemed to treat Mary brusquely. Yet even then she persevered in trusting faith, telling the servants to "do whatever he tells you" (John 2:5). At Jesus' farewell meal with his closest friends there was no place for his mother — though there was a place for her on Calvary. There, at the cross, Simeon's prophecy, that a sword would pierce Mary's heart, was fulfilled. Yet Mary went on trusting even when — as long ago — she "did not understand" (Luke 2:50).

Can there be any doubt that it is precisely this trusting faith of Mary's which we need amid the perplexities of our own day? Which of us can possibly understand all the upheavals we are witnessing in our world, and even in the Church? Today, especially, we need the trusting faith of Mary, who continued to trust when she did not understand.

Can there be any doubt that this faith will be granted to us in the measure in which we invoke the prayer of this woman who is the pattern of faith, and whom Jesus gave as mother to his best friend — and so to *all* his friends — as he died on the cross? (See John 19:26.) Can we doubt that Mary's faith will be granted to us as we continue to pray the age-old prayer based on the angel's words to Mary in today's Gospel?

Hail Mary, full of grace, the Lord is with you.
Blessed are you among women, and blessed is the fruit
of your womb, Jesus.
Holy Mary, Mother of God, pray for us sinners now and
at the hour of our death. Amen.

Christmas — Mass at Dawn

Titus 3:4-7; Luke 2:15-20

"THEY FOUND MARY AND JOSEPH, AND THE BABY
LYING IN THE MANGER."

- *To instill a sense of wonder and joy at the incarnation.*

The great religions of the world, someone has said, are all about the same thing: man's search for God. To this general statement there is an important exception. Christianity, and its parent Judaism, are concerned not with our search for God, but with *God's* search for *us*. Christmas is the time when we celebrate God's search, and his coming to us, in a special way. The readings at this Mass give us answers to three important questions about God's coming. They tell us *how* God comes, *when* he comes, and *why*.

1. *How does God come?* He comes in very ordinary and humble circumstances, to very ordinary and humble people.

There was nothing dramatic or unusual about the birth at Bethlehem. Few people took any notice. Those who did were either outsiders or eccentrics.

Shepherds were outsiders in the ancient world. Without any fixed abode, like gypsies today, they were mistrusted by respectable people. Since they frequently grazed their flocks on other people's lands they were considered too dishonest to be judges or witnesses in court. Their irregular lives made it impossible for them to observe the strict Sabbath and dietary laws. Hence shepherds were held in contempt by devout Jews.

The wise men, whose visit we commemorate at Epiphany, were eccentrics: astrologers of some kind from God knows where, who set off on a madcap journey following a star. We call them wise. To their contemporaries they were crackpots who were not playing with a full deck.

Nor were the surroundings of the birth at Bethlehem as attractive as we make them appear in our Christmas cribs. If Jesus were born today, it would probably be in a shack of corrugated iron or cardboard in Africa or Latin America, without electricity or inside plumbing — smelly, drafty, and cold.

How does God come? He comes in ordinary and humble surroundings, to people who live on the margin of society. That is how God came on the first Christmas. It is how he comes today.

2. *When does God come?* He comes when we least expect him — when people have given up expecting him altogether.

Matthew and Luke emphasize Jesus' descent from the great King David, and his birth "in David's city" (see Matthew 1:17, 20; Luke 1:27; 2:5, 11). This was to show that Jesus was the long-awaited Messiah, whose birth "of the house of David" the prophets had long foretold.

Almost six centuries before Jesus' birth, however, David's royal house had come to an end. The revival of his long-extinct dynasty after so long an interval was, humanly speaking, impossible. Moreover, the imperial census, which brought Joseph and Mary to Bethlehem, was a humiliating reminder that the nation over which David had ruled as the ideal king was now governed by a foreign emperor across the sea. Rome and not Jerusalem was the center of the world into which Jesus was born. At the very moment in which that world was set in motion by an imperial decree from its center, God was acting in an unimportant village on the edge of the empire in an event from which, two thousand years later, we continue to number our years.

34

Unthinkable? Impossible? Precisely! That is how God *normally* acts. He comes to us when we are least expecting him, when we have ceased expecting him at all. He comes in ways that stagger the imagination and demolish our conception of the possible. The creator of the universe comes as a tiny baby, born of a virgin.

3. *Why does he do it? Why does God come at all?*
Our second reading gives us the answer:

> When the kindness and love of God our Savior appeared, he saved us, not because of any righteous deeds we had done, but because of his mercy.

God's coming is not a reward for services rendered. He chose to come to us at the first Christmas for the same reason he comes to us today: not because we are good enough, but because *he* is so good, and so loving, that he wants to share his love with us, his unworthy, erring, and sinful children.

This explains too why he chose outsiders and eccentrics as the first witnesses of his coming. Before *him* we are *all* outsiders, *all* eccentrics. Before God we are all marginal, as the shepherds were and the wise men. It is his love, and his love alone, that draws us in from the darkness and coldness of the margin to the light and warmth of the center.

It is because God gave us his love at the first Christmas that we give gifts to one another at this season. The love God gave us then, and continues to give us today, is neither distant, nor abstract. God's love is a person who is very close to us. His name is Jesus Christ.

Feast of the Holy Family

Luke 2:22-40

"THE CHILD GREW."

> • *To show how Jesus, like us, first learned to love by being loved as a child; and to encourage the hearers to share their love with others.*

What do we know of Jesus' childhood and youth? Virtually nothing. Matthew records the flight of Mary and Joseph with their infant son into Egypt. Luke gives us the story we just heard in the Gospel, and another from Jesus' youth, when Mary and Joseph found their twelve-year-old son in the temple at Jerusalem after a three-day search. Apart from these incidents, the record is blank. No wonder that the first three decades of Jesus' life are called "the hidden years."

The obscurity surrounding Jesus' infancy and youth makes the words which conclude today's Gospel especially precious.

> The child grew in size and strength, filled with wisdom, and the grace of God was upon him.

Jesus' slow growth from infancy to manhood shows how completely he entered into our human condition. God could have sent his Son into the world already mature, in a way so dramatic as to compel everyone's attention. Instead Jesus made his entrance like every one of us, quietly, inconspicuously. Jesus passed through the weakness and vulnerability of infancy; through childhood, adolescence, and early manhood. At each stage Jesus possessed the perfection proper to that age. He was the perfect baby, the perfect boy, the perfect adolescent, the perfect young man. There was real growth, however: physical, mental, and also spiritual.

This growth took place in the context of a family: a family like any other, and yet also unlike any other. Luke introduces the members of this family at the beginning of today's Gospel, yet they speak no word throughout. Their silence is another aspect of those "hidden years."

Were those years really so hidden, however? Even if we have no record of them, is it not possible to reconstruct from our knowledge of Jesus' public ministry a little of what his first three decades must have been like? Perhaps you have heard the saying:

What a father says to his children is not heard by the world,
but it will be heard by posterity.

(Jean Paul Richter)

Many of Jesus' familiar sayings surely reflect the atmosphere of deep and simple trust in God, and undivided loyalty to him, which surrounded Jesus from birth. Is it fanciful to imagine Jesus first hearing in the carpenter's shop at Nazareth such words as these?

Do not be anxious about tomorrow; tomorrow will look after itself. Each day has troubles enough of its own.

(Matthew 6:34)

He who endures to the end will be saved.

(Mark 13:13; Matthew 10:22, 24:13)

The first shall be last, and the last shall be first.

(Matthew 19:30, 20:16; Mark 10:31; Luke 13:30)

Is it conceivable that any shoddy work came out of that carpenter's shop? That its customers were kept waiting for things beyond the time they were promised?

Father Theodore Hesburgh, president of the University of Notre Dame and one of our country's great priests, has said: "The most important thing a father can do for his children is to love their mother." Where did Jesus get his unsurpassed capacity to love even outcasts, lepers, beggars and hardened criminals if not from Joseph and Mary?

A recent television film on natural childbirth showed more clearly than many words the effect of a mother's love even in the first moments after birth. As the newborn baby was placed for the first time in its mother's arms, she cried out spontaneously: "O, you darling baby, I love you already!"

That is how each one of us learned to love: not from formal instruction or from books, but simply by *being* loved. Good parents do not wait until their children have done something to *deserve* parental love. Indeed, before birth, and for a long time thereafter, children are often so burdensome, especially to their mothers, that there is ample reason for their parents *not* to love them. Good parents love their children nevertheless.

It is our experience of this unconditional love that makes it possible for us, as we grow up, to love others in return. Jesus too learned to love in this way. Like every one of us, he first learned about God's love from experiencing the human love of Mary and Joseph.

Do you see now why the Church gives us, immediately after Christmas each year, this Sunday dedicated in a special way to the Holy Family? By recalling the atmosphere of love that surrounded Jesus from birth and molded him in that long process of human growth referred to in the final words of today's Gospel, we are reminded that this is the way each of *us* grew to maturity. This is the way *we* learned to love, if we have learned at all. This is the way we learned how much, and how unconditionally, God loves *us*.

One of the world's great lovers today is Mother Teresa. This diminutive woman who has renounced family, home, possessions — and in her late thirties the security of membership in a conventional religious order — has gained already the hundredfold reward that Jesus promises to those who renounce all for his sake (see Mark 10:30). Here is what Mother Teresa says about loving and being loved.

> The greatest suffering is being lonely, being unwanted, being unloved; just having no one, having forgotten what it is like to have the human touch, human love; what it is to be wanted, what it is to be loved, what it is to have your own people. The greatest diseases are not leprosy, tuberculosis, or cancer. A much greater disease is to be unwanted, to be unloved.

On this feast of the Holy Family God is asking each one of us whom he has already made members of his family in baptism, and whom he loves totally and unconditionally, to be *his* *agents* in loving the unloved, the unwanted, the unlovable. Here at his holy table Jesus Christ, God's Son, fills us with his love — so that we may go forth from here to *share* that love with others.

Solemnity of Mary, Mother of God

Galatians 4:4-7; Luke 2:16-21

NOT SLAVES, BUT SONS.

• *To help the hearers see that salvation is a free gift, not a reward.*

Few words strike such a sensitive nerve in people today as the term "liberation." For decades liberation from colonial rule and exploitation by richer and more powerful foreign countries has been a central concern of perhaps half the nations of the world. We read about black liberation, women's liberation, even about something called "liberation theology."

Liberation is Paul's theme in today's second reading. The purpose of Jesus' life, Paul writes, was "to deliver from the law those who were subjected to it, so that we might receive our status as adopted sons." If Paul were writing today he would add: "and daughters." Because of Jesus Christ's life, death, and resurrection, Paul says, "you are no longer a slave but a son!"

Christ has liberated us from what Paul calls slavery to the law: the Ten Commandments, plus the more than six hundred interpretations of them that had been developed by the rabbis by Paul's day. Paul found this legal system enslaving because it seemed to lay down the conditions he had first to fulfill before God would love him and bless him. How could we ever be sure that we had kept the law well enough to merit God's love? Paul asked. He confessed that as far as he was concerned, this certainly was unattainable. In his letter to the Romans, Paul wrote: "The good which I want to do I fail to do.

But what I do is the wrong which is against my will" (7:19).

Which of us could not say the same?

The heart of Paul's letter is the good news that God's love is *not* reserved for those who first prove they deserve it by fulfilling God's law. The idea that God would only love people who earned his love constituted "slavery" for Paul. Jesus had liberated us from this slavery, Paul taught, by making us his sisters and brothers, daughters and sons of his heavenly Father and ours.

> You are no longer a slave but a son; and if a son, then also by
> God's act an heir.

Sons and daughters do not have to earn their inheritance. It is theirs by right.

It is good to be reminded of this as we begin a new year. The basis of our relationship with God is not what *we* do for him, but *what God has already done for us* — not as a reward for services rendered, but simply out of love. This reminder is especially important for us because it cuts clean across the messages our society is constantly sending us.

The world in which we live tells us that we get ahead by achievement. Even as little children, our schoolteachers classify us as achievers or non-achievers. Later we may be rated as under-achievers and over-achievers. Society gives super-achievers the highest rewards: wealth, power, and fame. The important thing in life, we are constantly told, is to achieve as much as we possibly can.

This unceasing drive for achievement is a modern form of the "slavery" that Paul writes about in our second reading. God alone knows how much tension, and how many breakdowns in physical and mental health are caused today by people feeling pressured to ever higher levels of achievement.

How fitting, therefore, that the Church should dedicate this first day of the new year to a woman who is known not for what she achieved, but for what she *received*. "Mary treasured all these things and reflected on them in her heart," today's Gospel tells us. The things stored in Mary's heart were not what *she* did for God, but what *God* had done for *her*:

- that first visit of the angel with his overwhelming news;
- the beautiful and precious words of Mary's cousin Elizabeth: "when the sound of your greeting reached my ears, the baby leaped in my womb for joy" (Luke 1:44);
- the visit of the shepherds recounting the angels' message to them;
- and later the arrival of those strange "wise men from the east" with their remarkable tale of following a star (Matthew 2:2).

How much of that was Mary's achievement? None of it! It was all God's gift, sheer gift.

It was a happy inspiration that caused the revisers of the Church calendar a few years ago to place Mary at the gate of the new year. Mary is the model of Christian discipleship, the one who was always totally open to God's action in her.

Today's feast gives us the best of all new year's resolutions: to live as Mary did. Do not worry and fret about what you must do for God. Be open instead, as Mary was, to what God wants to do for you, in you, and through you for others. Then anything you do manage to do for God will be a *response* — your attempt to thank our loving heavenly Father who loves us with the tenderness and passion of a mother, and whose gifts and care always exceed by far all we can ever desire and deserve.

As you cross the threshold of the new year, treasure in your memory, as Mary did, all that God has done for you already: his unbelievable patience with you; his constant forgiveness of your sins; the preservation of your life amid so many dangers. Reflect on all three things in your heart, as Mary did.

If you do that — even if you just *try* to do that — then the year that is just one day old today will be what, deep in our hearts, we all hope and pray it will be: a truly *happy* new year.

Epiphany

Matthew 2:1-12

GOLD, FRANKINCENSE, AND MYRRH.

* *To proclaim Jesus' role as king, priest, and sacrifice, fore-shadowed in the Magi's gifts, as the model for our lives.*

Who were these "astrologers" anyway? Where did they come from? Where did they disappear to? We do not know. On the level of history the story in today's Gospel is shrouded in mystery. When we move to the *religious* level, however, the mystery falls away. The gifts offered by the wise men (to give them their more familiar name) tell us a great deal about the one to whom they were offered. They gave him:

* gold for a king;
* incense for a priest; and
* myrrh for his burial.

Jesus was a king. Yet Jesus was different from all other kings known to history. That is why he was reluctant to claim his royal title (see John 18:33-37). Unlike other kings, Jesus was never interested in amassing possessions and wealth. He had no palace, not even a fixed abode (see Luke 9:58). He never lorded it over people. Jesus was a *shepherd-king* who ruled by *serving*, even to the extent of sacrificing his own life (see John 10:11).

Jesus was also a priest. A priest is a man for others; a person set apart to offer God prayer, praise, and sacrifice on behalf of others. The smoke of incense curling its way heavenwards symbolizes this priestly activity. Judged by "results," burning incense is a sheer waste. So is prayer, if we are looking for measurable results. "How can you be sure anyone is listening?" a priest was asked as he prayed the Breviary, the Church's official offering of prayer and praise to God. Apart from faith, prayer *is* a waste. Without faith you cannot prove that anyone is listening. *With* faith, however, no proof is necessary.

Jesus exercised his priesthood in those many nights of solitary prayer we read about in the Gospels. He was also a priest, however, when he healed the sick, consoled sorrowers, and comforted people oppressed by suffering and sin. The supreme exercise of Jesus' priesthood came, however —

On the cross, where Jesus offered his heavenly Father not merely the prayer of his heart and lips, but his very life. To anyone without faith the cross is defeat and a scandalous waste. For those *with* faith, the cross is the place of victory. The most eloquent symbol of this victory is the empty tomb, which shows that the power of death and evil has been broken. Because of the sacrifice offered on Calvary by Jesus, our shepherd-king and priest, evil cannot control or master us without our consent.

The wise men's gifts foretold all this long beforehand: gold for a king, incense for a priest, and myrrh for his burial. Jesus shares these three functions with us. Paul calls Jesus "the eldest among a large family of brothers" (Romans 8:29). Each one of us became a member of this great family at baptism. We share the functions of Christ, our elder brother.

Like Christ, our shepherd-king, we too are called to *serve* others. This is Jesus' explicit command (see Luke 22:25f). The noblest of the pope's many titles is "Servant of the servants of God." Whenever popes have *lived* that title, and inspired others to similar lives of service, the Church has enjoyed spiritual health. Whenever popes and the Church have neglected their servant role, the Church has fallen sick, no matter how much wealth and power and prestige it may have enjoyed.

We share too in Christ's *priestly* function. Like him, we are to be people of prayer. Prayer is the soul's breath and food. Without prayer we sicken spiritually, and often physically as well. Like Jesus, we are called to bring the love, healing, and power of God to others. We do so not so much by words (for words are cheap), as by the force of our example (see Matthew 5:16 and 7:21-23).

Finally, we are called to share in Jesus' *death*. God asks us to die daily to the selfishness and self-centeredness that lurk within each of us. One day God will ask us to give back to him the precious gift of life itself, so that he can raise us to enjoy with Jesus, our elder brother, new eternal life with God: a life without suffering, without sorrow, without sin.

The wise men offered gold, frankincense, and myrrh: the best and most costly gifts they had. Somewhere in this church today someone is longing to do the same. Yet when you look at your own life you seem to have so little to offer the Lord: broken resolutions, compromised ideals, good that you might have done and failed to do, evil that you could have avoided and did not. You wanted to give Jesus so much. What you have actually given him seems too little. You ask yourself: What *can* I give him?

An English poet asked that question a century ago — and gave her own answer. It is beautiful. Listen.

> What can I give him, poor as I am?
> If I were a shepherd, I would bring a lamb;
> If I were a wise man, I would do my part;
> Yet what I can I give him — give my heart.
> (Christina Georgina Rossetti)

Baptism of the Lord

Isaiah 42:1-4, 6-7; Mark 1:7-11

JESUS' BAPTISM—AND OURS.

- *To show from Mark's description of Jesus' baptism the meaning of ours.*

"Who is this man?" This question, asked so often about Jesus by his contemporaries, still fascinates people today. Four details in Mark's description of Jesus' baptism, which we have just heard, help to tell us who Jesus is. These four details are deeply significant to anyone familiar, as Jesus himself was, with the Hebrew Scriptures. The four details are:

- the rending of the heavens,
- the descent of the Spirit,
- the hovering dove,
- the heavenly voice.

1. "Immediately on coming up out of the water [Jesus] saw the sky rent in two." Mark uses this dramatic expression to signal that Jesus' public ministry, which he is about to describe, will fulfill the prayer uttered long ago by the prophet Isaiah (64:1-4):

> Oh, that you would *tear the heavens* and come down ... to make known your name to your enemies, and make the nations tremble at your presence, working unexpected miracles such as no one has ever heard of before.

2. From the opening in the sky, Mark tells us, Jesus saw "the Spirit descending on him." These words evoke the opening of our first reading: "Here is my servant whom I uphold

47

. . . upon whom I have *put my spirit*." Jesus, according to Mark, fulfills Isaiah's prophecy about a coming "servant of the Lord."

He is the one upon whom God has put his Spirit; the one who will "bring forth justice to the nations," as Isaiah wrote. Jesus does not do this with the conventional means of power politics, however, but quietly: "not crying out, not shouting, not making his voice heard in the street." Jesus, in other words, acts upon people *inwardly*. He does not try to whip us up by propaganda, but gently molds us by the power of his example, wooing us with a love that will not let us go. Isaiah foretold this too in our first reading: "a bruised reed he shall not break, and a smoldering wick he shall not quench."

3. The descent of God's Spirit, Mark writes, was "like a dove." This image of a dove fluttering over Jesus' head as he emerged from the waters of the Jordan evokes a familiar verse at the beginning of the first creation story in Genesis: "Now the earth was a formless void, there was darkness over the deep, and God's spirit *hovered over the water*" (1:2).

Both at creation, and at Jesus' baptism, the "hovering" of God's spirit announced that the Lord of creation was at work, bringing light out of darkness and order out of chaos.

4. Finally there was the heavenly voice proclaiming: "You are my beloved Son. On you my favor rests." In our first reading Isaiah spoke of God's "servant." At Jesus' baptism the heavenly voice declared that he was more than a servant. He is God's "beloved Son."

Mark implies that Jesus alone perceived these four signs: the rending of the heavens, the descent of the Spirit, the hovering dove, and the heavenly voice. Together they disclose who Jesus is. His identity remained hidden from the onlookers, however, who did not perceive these signs. Mark records them in order to disclose Jesus' true identity. The whole of Jesus' public ministry, which Mark will now narrate, is intelligible only in the light of this mysterious event at the beginning, with its rich scriptural symbolism, which proclaims who Jesus is.

Mark had another reason for recording these four signs at Jesus' baptism. This reason is suggested in John's words beforehand: "I have baptized you in water; he will baptize you in the Holy Spirit." John's baptism imparted forgiveness; Jesus' baptism imparted power. At the Jordan Jesus received the Holy Spirit not just for himself, but in order to pass on this Spirit to others. To do so, however, Jesus would have to undergo what Jesus himself called another baptism: his baptism of blood on Calvary (see Luke 12:50). At his baptism in the River Jordan Jesus left behind his hidden life at Nazareth to embark on his public ministry. This ended at Calvary. From the garden tomb nearby Jesus rose in the power of the same Holy Spirit whom he had received in baptism, to impart this Spirit to all who would become his sisters and brothers in baptism.

When each of us was baptized there was (to use the language of Isaiah and Mark) a real "rending of the heavens." God's Spirit descended on each of us, to lead us from the darkness of sin into the light of God's love; to bring order out of the inevitable chaos of a life lived without God. Over each of us, at our baptism, God said: "This is my beloved son. This is my beloved daughter." That is not what we are striving to *become*. It is what we *already are*. That, and nothing less than that, is what God had already done for each of us.

The whole Christian life — all our striving, all our praying, every attempt to be generous with God and with others — is our attempt to *thank* God for our high destiny, and for his great gifts, so far beyond anything we deserve. That lived thanksgiving will be complete only when the Lord Jesus calls us home, to present us to his Father. When he does so he will repeat the words first spoken at our baptism: "This is my beloved son. This is my beloved daughter."

First Sunday in Lent

Mark 1:12-15

"HE STAYED IN THE WASTELAND FORTY DAYS."

* *By showing the spiritual strength Jesus gained through his testing in the desert, to encourage the hearers to make a fresh effort at prayer this Lent.*

Every detail in this brief Gospel reading is rich in biblical images, and rich too in spiritual significance. The passage is from the first chapter of Mark's Gospel, where it immediately follows the account of Jesus' baptism. There Jesus saw God's Spirit descending on him "like a dove" (vs. 10). Now this same Spirit sends Jesus "out towards the desert."

Jesus was experiencing one of life's basic laws. It is this. Every ascent to the spiritual heights is followed by a descent to the dark valley. We long to live on life's mountaintops, where we can sense God's nearness and the reality of the spiritual world. It cannot be. It would not be good for us, even if such a thing were possible.

Even Jesus could not remain always on the heights. The great spiritual experience of his baptism was followed at once by those forty days in the wilderness, "put to the test there by Satan," as Mark writes. We live by faith, not by sight. Faith is developed and deepened not on the mountaintops, but in the desert, when God seems to be absent, and silent.

Jesus' forty days "in the wasteland" remind us of the forty years Jesus' people, the Jews, spent wandering in the wilderness after their deliverance from slavery in Egypt. In those four decades those who had experienced their miraculous deliverance at the Red Sea had ample opportunity to wonder

51

whether it had really happened. Many of the people even longed for a return to the "good old days" back in Egypt. Meanwhile a new generation grew up which knew of God's wonderful intervention in their parents' lives only by hearsay.

Jesus' forty days alone in the wasteland gave him ample opportunity to doubt the reality of his great spiritual experience at Jordan. Had the Spirit really descended on him like a dove? Had he really heard the voice from heaven proclaiming him "my beloved Son"? Or was it all an illusion? Doubts such as these about his life's work were surely part of that testing by Satan of which we heard a moment ago in Mark's account.

Confronting such doubts was what gave Jesus his spiritual power. It was those forty days alone in the wasteland that enabled Jesus to say to rough fishermen shortly afterwards, "Come with me, and I will make you fishers of men" — and have them obey him on the spot (see Mark 1:17). It was in the solitude of the desert, "put to the test by Satan" and "with the wild beasts" (as Mark writes) that Jesus became the man of whom we read later in this same chapter: "And they were astonished at his teaching, for he taught them as one who had authority," and not like the other preachers they knew (1:22).

If you want to amount to anything in life (and which of us does not?), if you want to achieve something beyond the ordinary, then you must spend time in the desert. Show me someone who has left a mark on the world, in any age, in any field of endeavor — an artist, a thinker, a writer; a soldier, an explorer, an entrepreneur; a scientist, a prophet, a priest; a Francis of Assisi, a Mother Teresa, a Martin Luther King — and I will show you someone who has spent time in the desert. Silence, solitude, hard grinding work; weeks, perhaps years of being in the desert of loneliness, of seeming failure, where each successive glimpse of the cool refreshing waters of achievement and success turns out to be a mirage — that is the experience of all the great men and women of our race.

Perhaps you have seen the television film of Mother Teresa. In one scene she is sitting in an airplane, answering mail as she flies to open a new foundation for God's poor. "Mother, where do you get your energy?" someone asks. Mother Teresa's reply is as simple as it is unforgettable. "We begin every day with him, and end every day with him. That is the most beautiful thing."

Are you beginning and ending the day with Jesus Christ? Perhaps you have grown slack. If so, resolve this Lent to begin again. Between now and Easter make time and space in your life for him: not just at the beginning of the day and at the end, when you are tired and no longer able to concentrate. Decide to give Jesus Christ some time *during* the day. Turn off the radio and television. As you drive your car, or stand in the checkout line while shopping, during your lunch hour or another pause at work: turn to God, be silent, pray the rosary, read a few verses of Scripture. Or simply be still: Lift up your heart and mind with a few words, or none at all, to the source of your being, to your Savior, your Lord, your best friend.

Follow Jesus' invitation to join him in the desert, to "come with me . . . to some lonely place where you can rest quietly" (Mark 6:31). When you do, you will discover Jesus' desert secret:

They who wait upon the Lord will renew their strength:
they shall mount up with eagles' wings;
they shall run and not grow weary;
they shall walk and not faint.

(Isaiah 40:31)

Second Sunday in Lent

Mark 9:2-10

"THIS IS MY SON ... LISTEN TO HIM."

• *To explain the meaning of Jesus' transfiguration and the importance of listening for Jesus' words in everyday life.*

Few incidents in the Gospels are so difficult to speak about as the one we have just heard described in today's Gospel. Like Jesus' resurrection, of which we have no description at all, the transfiguration is a mystery. It yields its secret only if we respect the mystery. The gospel writer, Mark, does so by describing the transfiguration in *symbols*.

The unnamed "high mountain" is itself such a symbol. In the thought-world of the Bible, mountains symbolized remoteness from ordinary worldly affairs, and nearness to God. Moses received the Ten Commandments on Mt. Sinai. Elijah, who appears with Moses on the mountain of Jesus' transfiguration, experienced the climax of *his* career on Mt. Carmel (see 1 Kings 18). Jesus ascended a mountain to call his twelve apostles (Mark 3:13). He withdrew to a mountain to pray following the feeding of the five thousand in the wilderness (John 6:15).

The dazzling whiteness of Jesus' clothes symbolizes the brightness of God's glory, which no mortal can look upon and live (see Exodus 33:20-23). The Book of Revelation uses this same symbolism when it says that in heaven the blessed will be "robed all in white" (3:5).

Elijah and Moses, the two greatest heroes of Jesus' people, symbolize the special relationship of the Jewish people with God. Together they point to Jesus as the one who fulfills all his people's hopes and expectations. Jesus is greater than either of them, greater even than Moses and Elijah together.

Peter is so fascinated by this wonderful experience that he wants to prolong it. The three "booths" or tents that Peter wants to erect are reminiscent of the Jewish Feast of Booths, a joyful autumn celebration that recalled the time when God's people lived in tents during their desert wanderings. The Feast of Booths looked forward to the joy of the end-time when God would visit his people and complete the blessings promised in the covenant he had made with Moses in the wilderness.

Peter's suggestion, that they prolong the dazzling vision by erecting three booths for Jesus and his two visitors from beyond the grave, is immediately followed by the descent of the cloud. This is the most striking symbol of all. Repeatedly in Scripture the cloud is the symbol of God's presence (see Exodus 24:15ff; Acts 1:9). The voice from the cloud speaks the same words uttered at Jesus' baptism: "This is my Son, my beloved." Here, however, the words are addressed not to Jesus, but to his disciples. The concluding words, "Listen to him," remind us of Moses' prophecy: "The Lord your God will raise up a prophet from among you like myself, and you shall listen to him" (Deuteronomy 18:15).

The transfiguration's meaning can never be fully explained. The biblical symbols used by Mark in his account suggest deeper meanings impossible to state in a literal description. The transfiguration is a mystery because, though it happened in time, it comes from beyond time. For a brief moment, there on the mountain, the veil between time and eternity, between earth and heaven, was lifted. Jesus' three friends caught a momentary glimpse of the invisible, spiritual world of God.

The concluding words, "Listen to him," express the significance of this mystery for Jesus' friends: not only for the three present on the mountain with him, but for all the friends of Jesus, ourselves included.

We, the friends and followers of Jesus Christ, are the company of those who listen to his words. Jesus does not grant us, any more than he granted to Peter, James, and John, the continuous vision of his glory. We live not on the mountaintop of great spiritual experiences, but in the valley of life's ordinary duties. There we do not look for dazzling visions from beyond. Instead we listen for Jesus' voice.

Jesus speaks to us in many ways: in the Holy Scriptures, in the teaching of his Church, through the circumstances of daily life, in the promptings of conscience, and in the needs of those we encounter along life's way. In the world to come it will be different. There we shall *see* the Lord. In this world, however, we live by faith, and not by sight.

This is the way Jesus lived. How bitterly his faith was tested as he passed through death's dark valley we learn from his anguished cry on the cross: "My God, my God, why have you forsaken me?" (Matthew 27:46). Jesus summons us to follow him on the way of the cross: to endure whatever trials and sufferings life may bring. The way of the cross will lead us, as it led Jesus, through suffering to death. But beyond death for us, as for him, is resurrection to life eternal. Then faith will give way to sight. Then our earthly pilgrimage between a mostly overcast sky will yield to the uninterrupted vision of God's glory. We shall have reached our true homeland, that heavenly city which needs neither sun nor moon, "for the glory of God gives it light, and the lamp is the Lamb" (Revelation 21:23).

Now, however, is the time not for seeing, but for hearing. We listen for the Father's voice and heed his command, as he speaks to us the words first uttered to those three friends of Jesus on the mountain two thousand years ago:

"This is my Son, my beloved. Listen to him."

Third Sunday in Lent

1 Corinthians 1:22-25; John 2:13-25

"WE PREACH CHRIST CRUCIFIED."

• *To show that Jesus, who overturned the tables of the money changers in the temple, also overturns our ideas and expectations, replacing them with "the folly of the Cross."*

Was Jesus always meek and mild? To judge by the gospel reading we have just heard, he could also be angry, even violent. Why? There is no suggestion that the money changers whose tables Jesus overturned were corrupt. In fact, both they and the people who sold the animals used in the temple sacrifices performed useful and necessary functions. To understand why Jesus was angry, we must turn back to the criticism the Jewish prophets had repeatedly made of the way their people worshiped God. In cleansing the temple Jesus was acting out this criticism in a particularly dramatic way.

Amos, for instance, the first of the writing prophets, represents God as saying to the people of his day: "I hate, I spurn your pilgrim feasts; I will not delight in your sacred ceremonies. When you present your sacrifices and offerings I will not accept them" (5:21).

Repeatedly the prophets emphasized that what God wanted was not the offering of *things*. God desired the hearts and minds of those who worshiped him. To come before God with long prayers and material offerings, whether of money or anything else, and then to live a life which was disobedient to God's law, cheating, lying, stealing and oppressing the poor: that was worse than useless, the prophets said. It cried to heaven for vengeance. This was the consistent message of all

58

the prophets. (See Hosea 6:6; Isaiah 1:11-17; Micah 6:6-8; Jeremiah 7:21-23.)

This prophetic demand for pure, disinterested worship was the background for Jesus' cleansing of the temple. In a dramatic way he was reminding people that worship could never be a form of barter or bargaining with God. We do not worship God to earn a reward. Worship is something we owe to God *apart* from any thought of reward.

What a lesson there is there for us Catholics! We owe God our worship at Mass on Sunday, as well as the worship of obedience to him in daily life, simply because God has made us. God has given us all we are and have, sin excepted. One day we shall have to give an accounting of how we have used the gifts God has lavished upon us. We owe God our worship because his Son Jesus has paid with his life's blood the price of our sins.

The gospel writer was referring to Jesus' death when he quoted the words of Psalm 69: "Zeal for your house consumes me." On the surface the words seem to refer to Jesus' zeal for the offering of pure, spiritual worship in the temple, which was the earthly dwelling place, or house, of his heavenly Father. But the words have a deeper meaning. Jesus' zeal for pure worship in his Father's house would consume him in a more literal sense. It would lead to his crucifixion. Enraged by Jesus' attack on their religious institutions, the spiritual leaders of the people delivered him to death.

Jesus was also referring to his death when he spoke of the temple being destroyed and "raised up" in three days. His hearers naturally assumed that he was talking about the building where they were standing. Jesus actually meant the destruction of his own body. As Son of God he was himself the dwelling place of God in a way that no building of wood or stone could ever be. After Jesus was raised from death on the third day, the gospel writer informs us, his friends recalled these words of the Master and for the first time understood their true import.

Jesus' action in overturning the tables of the money changers was typical of his whole message and ministry. Jesus is constantly overturning worldly standards and expectations. This is Paul's theme in today's second reading. People who demand a "sign" before they will believe, Paul writes there, find this demand overturned by Jesus Christ. He does not offer us any sign strong enough to compel faith. The empty tomb, and the appearances of the risen Lord, were Jesus' strongest signs. Neither at the time, nor since, did they bring to faith anyone who was not already open to faith in Jesus.

It is the same, Paul writes, with people who come to Jesus expecting to be impressed by some special "wisdom": subtle arguments and deep philosophy. They too find their expectations overturned. Instead of wisdom Jesus Christ offers what Paul calls the folly of the Cross: the symbol not of success, but of humiliating failure.

Paul's message is the message of Jesus himself. "We preach Christ crucified," Paul writes. A crucified Lord drives out the longing we all have for a success story, as surely as Jesus drove from his Father's house those who were encouraging people to use worship, which is the offering of grateful praise to God, as a means of barter with God.

To all those who are willing to have their ideas and expectations and demands overturned, however, this crucified Lord is

the power of God and the wisdom of God. For God's folly is wiser than men, and his weakness more powerful than men.

Fourth Sunday in Lent

Ephesians 2:4-10; John 3:14-21

"GOD SO LOVED THE WORLD."

• *To proclaim God's unconditional love, and to appeal for a response.*

At the center of every Catholic Church in the world you will find a cross. The cross hangs around the necks of hundreds of thousands of people in our world who give no other outward sign of being religious. Teachers of young children report that when they show their pupils a selection of holy cards and ask them to choose one, the children will almost always choose the card with the picture of Jesus on the cross.

Why is the cross so important, and so central? Why, after two thousand years, has it lost none of its fascination and power? The best answer is simply this: because the cross is a picture of *how much God loves us.* "There is no greater love than this," Jesus tells us, "that a man should lay down his life for his friends" (John 15:13).

"God so loved the world that he gave his only Son," we heard in the Gospel. It was the most God had to give. That is why the cross is at the center of every Catholic Church in the world. That is why the cross is also at the center of the Church's preaching. Often when we hear the words "preaching" or "sermon" we think of a long list of do's and don'ts: all the things we must first do or avoid before God will love us and bless us. Is that good news — to be told that God will not love us until we have demonstrated that we are worthy of his love? That is not good news. That is horribly bad news.

61

The good news of the Gospel is that God loves us *right now*. That is Paul's message in the second reading:

God is rich in mercy; because of his great love for us [not because of our love for him] he brought us to life with Christ *when we were dead in sin*. . . . It is owing to his favor that salvation is yours through faith. This is not your doing, it is God's gift; neither is it a reward for anything you have accomplished.

Does this mean that our obedience to God's law is unimportant? Of course not. It is vitally important. God's laws tell us how we should *respond* to the free gift of God's love. But the preaching of the law alone has little power to convert people. It is *love* that breaks through the hardened sinner's heart. Here is an example — a kind of modern parable.

Minnie is eighty-seven years old and a widow. She has lived for several years in a nursing home. It is hard to grow old and have to give up your own place. Minnie hasn't adjusted to the loss of her independence yet. She is crabby and disagreeable much of the time. She complains over trifles. She criticizes those who look after her, often for no reason at all.

One day Minnie received a letter from her great-grandson at college. He told her how much the whole family loved her, how in her old age she was an inspiration to them. He said how much he admired her. When the chaplain at the home came to visit Minnie, he found her clutching the letter, in tears.

"I want you to read that, Father," Minnie said. When he had, she told the priest she wanted to make her confession. She did so and received the Lord's forgiveness: that love that will not let go, which heals us and makes us well again.

Afterwards Minnie was transformed. For the first time in weeks she was kind to the nurses. Instead of criticizing them, she thanked them for all they did for her. What had changed her was a letter that simply said: "Grandma, we love you." It is love that breaks through.

The cross is a picture of *God's* love for us. Listen again to the words of the Gospel:

> Just as Moses lifted up the serpent in the desert, so must the Son of Man be lifted up, that all who believe may have eternal life in him. Yes, God so loved the world that he gave his only Son, that whoever believes in him may not die, but may have eternal life. God did not send the Son into the world to condemn the world, but that the world might be saved through him.

The One who hangs on the cross, to show us God's love, says elsewhere in this fourth Gospel: "I am the light of the world" (8:12). In today's Gospel he tells us that our eternal destiny is being determined even now, by how we react to his light.

> Everyone who practices evil hates the light; he does not come near it for fear his deeds will be exposed. But he who acts in truth comes into the light, to make clear that his deeds are done in God.

Are *you* walking in the bright light of Jesus' love? Or do you fear his light because of what it might reveal in the dark corners of your life which you try desperately to keep hidden? Now, in this hour, Jesus Christ is inviting you to put away fear. Come into the bright sunshine of his love. Once you do, the fire of Christ's love will burn out in you everything that is opposed to his light. Then you will have no reason for fear.

Then you will have no need to hide. You will be home. You will be safe: for this life, but also for eternity.

> Whoever believes in him avoids condemnation, but whoever does not believe is already condemned for not believing in the name of God's only Son. The judgment in question is this: The light came into the world, but men loved darkness rather than light because their deeds were wicked.

The eternal destiny of each one of us is being determined by our response to the light, and love, of Jesus Christ. He is waiting for *your* response, right now.

Fifth Sunday in Lent

Hebrews 5:7-9; John 12:20-33

NO CROSS, NO CROWN.

* *To proclaim the power of the Cross.*

> In the days when Christ was in the flesh, he offered prayers
> and supplications with loud cries and tears to God, who was
> able to save him from death.

These words from today's second reading refer to Jesus'
anguish in the face of death. John's Gospel, from which today's gospel reading is taken, contains no account of Jesus'
agonized prayer in the garden of Gethsemane the night before
he died. Instead it has Jesus' prayer in the upper room. We
heard a portion of it a few minutes ago.

> My soul is troubled now, yet what should I say — Father, save
> me from this hour? But it was for this that I came to this hour.
> Father, glorify your name!

Jesus' humanity was not a disguise that he put on for the
period of his earthly life to conceal his true nature as God's
Son. Jesus really experienced what we experience, and suffered as we suffer. Before the encounter with the Samaritan
woman at the well, Jesus was tired from a long journey on
foot (see John 4:6). He wept at the death of his dear friend
Lazarus (John 11:35). And as he stood on the threshold of a
painful death, Jesus felt the intense anguish that any of us
would experience in such a desperate situation.

With all the fervor of which he was capable Jesus prayed
for deliverance — yet went beyond this prayer to ask that he

not be delivered from death, should his acceptance of death be the means of glorifying his heavenly Father's name. That prayer is part of what our second reading referred to when it spoke of Jesus offering "prayers and supplications with loud cries and tears to God, who was able to save him from death." The writer adds: "And he was heard because of his reverence."

Was Jesus' prayer heard? Is not the Cross proof that his prayer was *not* heard — or at least not granted? So it would seem. In reality, however, the Cross is not the place of Jesus' final defeat, but of his ultimate triumph. Jesus confessed his faith in this victory when he said in today's Gospel: "Now will this world's prince be driven out." It was "this world's prince" — Satan, or the personification of evil — who brought Jesus to the Cross. But in this passage Jesus confessed his faith that Satan's seeming triumph would be an illusion. The empty tomb of Easter showed that the victor in the cosmic conflict on Calvary was not the "prince of this world," but Jesus Christ.

The price of that victory was Jesus' death. Jesus explained this dark mystery by saying that even nature taught the same lesson.

> Unless the grain of wheat falls to the earth and dies, it remains just a grain of wheat. But if it dies, it produces much fruit.

We are part of that fruit — a portion of that great harvest which Jesus sowed when, on Calvary, he cast the precious seed of his own life into the soil of that earth, for love of which he had been born at Bethlehem some thirty years before. That we are Catholic Christians twenty centuries later, in a land and continent undreamed of in Jesus' day, is proof that Jesus

66

spoke true when he said: "I — once I am lifted up from earth — will draw all men to myself."

Jesus voluntarily laid down his life that we might live. He cast the seed of his life into the soil of Calvary to sow the rich harvest of which we are now a part. He summons us to live as he lived.

> If anyone would serve me, let him follow me; where I am, there will my servant be.

Where *is* Jesus Christ today? He is in every place of human need. Jesus is with the suffering: with the victims of poverty, oppression, war, and the hatreds that lead to war. Jesus is in ghettos, in prisons, especially in the cells on death row. He is with the victims of every kind of injustice. He is with *us* when we experience need or suffering of any kind: sickness, loneliness, injustice, bereavement, and bitter despair.

In the resurrection Jesus passed beyond all these things — as we too shall do one day when God raises us from death to eternal life with him. But because Jesus really tasted human suffering in all its anguish, he can understand and help us when we must suffer. Listen to the words that immediately precede our second reading (Hebrews 4:15-16). Jesus, we read there, "is not a high priest unable to sympathize with our weaknesses, but one who, because of his likeness to us, has been tested every way, as we are, only without sin. Let us therefore boldly approach the throne of the gracious God, where we may receive mercy and in his grace find timely help."

Continuing that thought, today's second reading calls Jesus "the source of eternal salvation for all who obey him." Obeying Jesus means following him. Jesus tells us in the Gospel what this means.

The man who loves his life loses it, while the man who hates his life in this world preserves it to life eternal. If anyone would serve me, let him follow me; where I am, there will my servant be.

That is easy to say. It is difficult to do. Mostly we want the crown without the Cross. We want Easter without Good Friday. That was impossible for Jesus. It is equally impossible for us. Jesus never promised to protect us from all suffering, and certainly not from the final suffering of death. He does promise, however, to be with us *in* every suffering, and to accompany us in the final suffering of our own personal death.

The guarantee that Jesus keeps this promise is the Cross — and behind the Cross the empty tomb.

Passion (Palm) Sunday

Mark 14:1-15:47

THE CENTRALITY OF THE CROSS.

- *To help the hearers meditate on the Cross.*

Bible scholars tell us that the passion narratives were the first parts of the Gospels to be written down. From the start the Christian community wanted to preserve faithfully every detail of the Lord's suffering and death. Mark's Gospel, from which the narrative we have just heard is taken, does not even mention Jesus' birth and infancy. Yet Mark devotes approximately a fifth of his Gospel to Jesus' passion. For him, as for the other three evangelists, the Cross was central.

Take the Cross out of our religion, and there is little left. The late Archbishop Fulton J. Sheen illustrated this truth with a personal experience. In his posthumously published autobiography, *Treasure in Clay,* Sheen told about a Jewish jeweler in New York City whom he knew for many years. One day the man phoned Bishop Sheen and asked him: "Would you like a large number of silver crucifixes?"

When the bishop called at the shop the jeweler showed him a little brown bag with dozens of silver crucifixes about four inches high.

"Where did you get them?" he asked the jeweler.

"From Catholic Sisters," the man replied. "They brought them in to me and said they were not going to use them any more. Wearing the crucifix separated them from the world. They wanted to know how much I would give them for the silver."

The jeweler added: "I weighed them out thirty pieces of silver. *What is wrong with your church?*"

"Just that!" Bishop Sheen replied. "The contempt of Christ and his cross which makes it worldly."

Fulton Sheen would not have been the man he was if he had not concluded the story by writing: "Those words became the channel of the Holy Spirit working in his soul. I explained to him the cost of redemption, the blood of Christ. He embraced the faith, and died in it."*

To learn the deepest meaning of our holy faith, we must take our stand beneath the cross of Jesus Christ. All the great lessons of life are learned at the foot of the cross.

---

*Cited from *Treasure in Clay: The Autobiography of Fulton J. Sheen* (New York, 1980) pp. 275f.

Easter Sunday

Acts 10:34a,37-43; John 20:1-9

THE GROUNDS OF OUR EASTER FAITH.

• *To show that the preaching of the Resurrection is not based on "tales artfully spun" (2 Peter 1:16), but on solid evidence.*

Nothing in our whole Christian faith is so crucial as the resurrection of Jesus Christ. If Jesus rose from the dead, everything in his life makes sense. If Jesus rose from the dead, life makes sense for us too, despite all the suffering and evil in the world and the certainty of death. If Jesus Christ did *not* rise from the dead, his life was at best a case of noble self-sacrifice; at worst a tragic waste. If Jesus did not rise from the dead, our lives too are tragic and ultimately meaningless.

For the truth of the Resurrection there is evidence of three kinds:

• the empty tomb;

• the appearances of the risen Lord; and —

• the Church's continuing experience of Jesus not as a dead hero, but as its living Lord.

1. *The empty tomb.*

The Gospel we have just heard tells us that the empty tomb was discovered by Mary Magdalene alone, "early in the morning ... while it was still dark." The other three Gospels say that the discovery was made by several women, after sunrise. These differences in the accounts are actually more true to life than separate narratives agreeing in all details. In a court of law, eyewitnesses seldom agree about all the details. It is perjurers who harmonize their stories in advance, to give them greater credibility.

Despite disagreement about how many people discovered the empty tomb, and when, all four Gospels report that the first witnesses were women. This is significant. In New Testament times the testimony of women had no legal force. Had the gospel writers made up the story of the empty tomb, they would not have cited as witnesses people whose testimony was not recognized by the laws of evidence then prevailing.

The empty tomb itself, however, does not prove the Resurrection. It could have been empty because the body was stolen. Matthew's Gospel reports that people at the time who wished to disprove the Resurrection claimed precisely that: Jesus' disciples had made off with his dead body, and then claimed he had risen (see Matthew 28:13-15). If we accept this, however, we must believe that the entire preaching of the early Church was based upon a known but carefully concealed fraud; and that those responsible for this fraud were prepared to die for it. If you believe that, you will believe anything.

Only one person in the New Testament believed in Jesus' resurrection on the evidence of the empty tomb alone. This was the anonymous disciple identified in today's Gospel as "the one Jesus loved." It was the special bond of love between this disciple and the Master that enabled this follower of Jesus to believe in the Resurrection before everyone else. This same unique love would permit this "disciple whom Jesus loved" to recognize the risen Lord before all the others when they were fishing at the sea of Tiberias, and Jesus stood on the shore at dawn (see John 21:7). All the other disciples came to believe in Jesus' resurrection not on the basis of the empty tomb, but only through the second kind of evidence for the Easter event —

2. *The appearances of the risen Lord.*

Jesus appeared after his resurrection only to those who had previously known him, loved him, and believed in him. As Peter said in our first reading, Jesus was seen "not by all, but only by such witnesses as had been chosen beforehand by God — by us who ate and drank with him after he rose from the dead."

In none of the resurrection appearances is there any evidence of halucination or wish-fulfillment. On the contrary, in every case those to whom Jesus appeared were initially skeptical or fearful, as if they were seeing a ghost. Only reluctantly and slowly did they come to believe that it was truly the Master they had known, alive again in flesh and blood.

This slowness of the witnesses to believe was due not only to the astonishing nature of the occurrence itself (for in human experience the dead do not come back to life). It was due also to a mysterious alteration in Jesus' appearance. He had not returned to the old life. That ended on Calvary. Jesus was raised to a *new* life, beyond death. His appearance was changed. The mode of his existence was changed. He could appear and disappear at will.

The empty tomb is the first evidence for Jesus' resurrection. In itself, however, the empty tomb proved only that Jesus' body was elsewhere. Save for the one disciple who was linked to Jesus by a special bond of love, none of his friends came to faith in the resurrection on the basis of the empty tomb alone. They were convinced only when they saw the risen Lord, talked with him, and ate with him.

Had there been no further evidence for Jesus' resurrection, we would expect his friends to become increasingly skeptical as the memory of their encounters with the risen Lord faded into the ever more distant past. In fact, precisely the opposite happened. In time Jesus' friends became not less, but *more* certain of the Resurrection. This growing certainty can be explained only by the third kind of evidence for Jesus' resurrection —

3. *The Church's continuing experience of Jesus not as a dead hero but as its living Lord.*

This evidence for Jesus' resurrection is available to us today. We cannot see the empty tomb. We have not seen the risen Lord. Nor can we listen to the testimony of those who have seen him. But we are members of that great company of people called the Catholic Church who experience Jesus not as a figure from the distant past, but as someone gloriously alive today. We experience him in this way especially when we obey Jesus' command at the last supper to "do this in my memory."

If Jesus were a dead hero from the distant past, the celebration of the eucharistic memorial which he left us would be an act of sadness. Always and everywhere, however, when Christians have "done this" in Jesus' memory, they have been filled with joy. We express our joy today in the Church's characteristic Easter greeting: "Alleluia!" This untranslatable word expresses more fittingly than a word of known meaning something that is, at bottom, inexpressible: our overwhelming joy at knowing that the One whom we here encounter is *not* a dead hero, but our ever present and risen Lord, gloriously alive for evermore, risen from the tomb bearing "the keys of death and death's domain," as we read in the Book of Revelation (1:18).

This joyful encounter with the risen Lord is the continuation not merely of the Last Supper, but of the meals which Jesus shared with his friends *after* his resurrection. Peter referred to those meals in our first reading, when he told how Jesus appeared to "us who ate and drank with him after he rose from the dead."

Because Jesus Christ is alive, we can live in confidence, in joy, in hope. The darkness of this age has been overpowered by the light of Him who is the world's light. The power of evil, evident in each day's headlines and in the evening news on television, is temporary. In raising his Son from death, God has shown that *his* power is *stronger* than evil. This world with all its horrors is still God's world. Death, our final enemy, is not the end. The grave, which was for Jesus only a temporary resting place on the way to a new and more glorious life, will be for us too the gateway to this same eternal life.

Truly we have every reason to join in the Church's ecstatic Easter hymn:

> This is the day the Lord has made:
> let us rejoice and be glad in it. Amen.

Second Sunday of Easter

John 20:19-31

OUR SUNDAY CELEBRATION.

- *To help the hearers see that the Sunday Eucharist is not merely an obligation but a celebration.*

"At the sight of the Lord the disciples rejoiced."

If a stranger who knew nothing about Christianity or Catholicism were to visit us at this Mass, would the visitor be struck by *our* joy? Joy is supposed to be a distinguishing mark of the followers of Jesus Christ. Why is it so often difficult to find in Catholic churches?

There are many reasons. One is the emphasis in Catholic teaching on the *obligation* of attending Sunday Mass. Many Catholics come to Mass on Sunday for this reason alone: to fulfill a legal obligation. For such people attending Sunday Mass is like paying an insurance premium. Like most insurance premiums, this one is paid with little joy and perhaps even a certain amount of resentment, simply because it is too dangerous to be without it, and you never know when you might need it.

This is no reason to question the obligation. It is important. We *need* obligations to bridge the valleys in life, when zeal and enthusiasm slacken. Things done solely to fulfill an obligation, however, are usually done with little joy. How much joy would there be in a marriage, for instance, in which the spouses thought only of their mutual obligations? In which they never did anything out of *love*, just to make each other happy?

Sunday Mass is so much more than an obligation. It is meant to be a *celebration*. Today's Gospel tells us how Jesus celebrated the first two Sundays after his resurrection, with his closest friends. On the "evening of the first day of the week," the Sunday of the Lord's resurrection, seeing Jesus was the *last* thing his frightened friends were expecting. After the tragedy of Calvary had come the report that Jesus' body was no longer in its final resting place. Terrified of what fresh disaster awaited them, they had locked the doors of the room where they met.

How filled with joy Jesus must have been at being able to surprise his friends! Even the locked door was no barrier to him now. Jesus had not been brought back to the old life. He had been raised to a new and higher life. He was no longer subject to the old restrictions of time and space. Jesus returned "a week later," in the same room. Again it was the first day of the week, a Sunday.

Jesus' first words to his frightened friends were: "Peace be with you." "Shalom — peace" is a conventional Jewish greeting, even today. Jesus meant far more, however, than merely an end to care and worry. Before his crucifixion Jesus had told his friends: "Peace is my parting gift to you, my own peace, such as the world cannot give" (John 14:27). Jesus gives a peace that comes from *outside* this world: from God. This peace is available to those — and only to those — who enter into a relationship of loving trust in Jesus Christ (see Luke 19:42; Ephesians 2:14,17).

Having fulfilled his promise to give his friends a peace not of this world, Jesus then gave them something more: a share in his own sending — a commission. Jesus did not intend the peace he gave only for those who received it. He wanted them to *share* this peace with others. Hence he told them: "As the Father has sent me, so I send you."

77

To help these friends of his carry out this mission, Jesus gave them yet another gift: his Holy Spirit. He did this by breathing on them, imitating God's action in creating new life (see Genesis 2:7; Ezekiel 37:9; Wisdom 15:11). With this gift of his Spirit Jesus bestowed also the power to forgive sins.

Every one of these things is repeated each time that we, the Lord's people, gather on this first day of the week to fulfill his command: "Do this in my memory" (1 Corinthians 11:24). Jesus comes to us, as he came to his frightened friends in that locked upper room in Jerusalem, in all the joy of his resurrection. He gives us, as he gave them, his peace: that peace which the world cannot give; the peace of those who enter into a relationship of loving trust in him, the risen Lord. We recall this gift in every Eucharist in the prayer after the Our Father: "Lord Jesus Christ, you said to your apostles, I leave you peace, my peace I give you. . ." Immediately we exchange a sign of this peace with one another.

In Holy Communion we are strengthened by the Lord's Body and Blood, made present under the signs of bread and wine through the power of his Holy Spirit. And at the close of the Mass Jesus sends us forth to a spiritually hungry world to share with others the peace, and the forgiveness, which he has given us here.

Those first friends of Jesus rejoiced to see him alive again, and to hear once more his familiar voice. For us who cannot see or hear Jesus Christ, save with the eyes and ears of faith, Jesus has a special blessing *not* given to those first friends of his. It is contained in Jesus' closing words in today's Gospel. Jesus addresses these words to us at this celebration today:

"Blest are you who have not seen, and have believed."

Third Sunday of Easter

Acts 3:13-15, 17-19; 1 John 2:1-5a; Luke 24:35-48

REDEMPTIVE SUFFERING.

- *To proclaim the atonement and to challenge the hearers to a decision based upon it.*

"You put to death the authors of life," Peter declared in today's first reading. We come closer to Luke's original text if we translate: "the leader to life." That was a title Peter's hearers recognized instantly. It referred to Moses. He was the leader to life who had led their forefathers to safety when they were trapped between the advancing army of the Egyptians and the impassable waters of the Red Sea.

Now, Peter told his people, God had given them a new leader to life. To emphasize the link with Moses, Peter used the same divine titles Moses had heard when he encountered God at the burning bush: "the God of Abraham, the God of Isaac, the God of Jacob" (Exodus 3:6). This same God, Peter declared, "the God of our fathers, has glorified his servant Jesus." Every one of Peter's hearers knew by that time the evidence for that glorification. It was the empty tomb of Easter morning. "You put to death the leader to life," Peter said boldly. "But God raised him from the dead, and we are his witnesses." All this had happened, Peter added, "to fulfill what God announced long ago through all the prophets: that the Messiah would suffer."

That was the boldest assertion of all. For it invited the rejoinder: "*When* did God announce that his Messiah would suffer?" The customary idea of the Messiah was that he would be

79

mighty and powerful, leading God's people to even greater triumphs than they had experienced under Moses. Nowhere do the Hebrew Scriptures contain a clear prediction that the Messiah would suffer. Only in the so-called Suffering Servant passages of Isaiah was such a thing even suggested. People were not at all sure, however, what those passages meant. And when Jesus applied them to himself, people did not understand him.

In another way, however, the Hebrew Scriptures *do* predict a suffering Messiah. They do so by showing that suffering is the lot of all those whom God calls to serve him in special ways. Moses, and all the prophets, encountered the same suspicion, jealousy, rejection, and persecution experienced by Jesus.

From the purely human point of view, those sufferings of God's servants were unrelieved tragedy. But it is part of the good news of the Gospel that God can transform tragedy into triumph. "You put to death the leader to life," Peter declared. No sooner had he stated this tragedy, however, than he announced its reversal: "But God raised him from the dead."

The Gospel tells us that the sufferings of God's chosen servant, the Messiah, are *not* unrelieved tragedy. "Jesus Christ," we heard in the second reading, "is an offering for our sins, and not for our sins only, but for those of the whole world." This truth, that the voluntary offering of his life by Christ on Calvary somehow makes up for the sins of the whole world, is a great mystery. On a lesser scale, however, we experience a similar transformation of evil through suffering whenever people give their lives in the struggle against the forces of darkness.

Our country's recent history gives us an example in Martin

Luther King, leading a nonviolent struggle for freedom and full citizenship for black Americans, only to be struck down by an assassin's bullet. His death did not overcome all prejudice. But it shocked thousands by revealing the depth of racial hatred which still exists in a nation that prides itself on being the land of the free and the home of the brave. Many who were formerly complacent or indifferent were moved by Martin Luther King's death to join the struggle for equal rights for all people, regardless of color.

In the Gospel we heard Jesus make the same affirmation advanced by Peter in the first reading. To his frightened friends Jesus said:

> It is written that the Messiah must suffer and rise from the dead on the third day. In his name repentance for the forgiveness of sins is to be preached to all nations, beginning at Jerusalem. You are witnesses of this.

Jesus addresses those same words to his friends throughout history. He is speaking them to us in this church right now. *We* are commissioned by the risen Lord to be witnesses both of his suffering, and of his resurrection. Jesus' suffering and death show what *we* do on our own, apart from God and in rebellion against God. The empty tomb of Easter shows that the worst we can do apart from God, and against God, can be, and is, overruled by God's power.

That contrast — on the one hand man organizing the world for himself, apart from God and against God, and on the other hand God's power overruling human rebellion and sin — challenges us to a decision. Will we stand with those who killed Jesus, the leader to life? Or will we recognize that though our own sins are part of the accumulated tale of evil which brought Jesus to the Cross, nevertheless he offered his life there for us too?

For those who desire it, there is forgiveness. For those who choose to stand on the side of Jesus, the leader to life, there is new life in this world, and in the world to come life eternal. Calvary is not the end. Behind the Cross is the empty tomb.

Fourth Sunday of Easter

Acts 4:8-12; 1 John 3:1-2; John 10:11-18

SALVATION IN THE NAME OF JESUS ALONE.

* *To help the hearers accept Christ's atoning love through faith,
and to show forth this love to others.*

Are the different religions simply alternative routes to the same goal? Many people believe they are. The Catholic Church disagrees. We take our stand with Peter, who in today's first reading boldly proclaims:

> There is no salvation in anyone else [than in Jesus Christ], for
> there is no other name in the whole world given to men by
> which we are to be saved.

How *are* you saved? The New Testament gives two different answers. It says that we are saved *only by love*. It also says that we are saved *only by faith*.

That we are saved *only by love* is Jesus' clear teaching in the parable of the sheep and the goats (Matthew 25:31-46). There Jesus says that in judgment only one standard will be applied. How much, or how little, have we done for people in need? Jesus said the same when asked what was the greatest commandment: Everything depends on *active love* of God and neighbor (see Matthew 22:35-40). Even the practice of religion will not save us without love, Jesus says. "Not everyone who says to me, 'Lord, Lord' will enter the kingdom of heaven, but only those who do the will of my heavenly Father" (Matthew 7:21).

Paul says the same: "The whole law is summed up in love" (Romans 13:10).

Yet the New Testament also tells us that *no one really loves enough to be saved.* "When you have done all that is commanded of you," Jesus says (and which of us has?), "you should say: 'We are servants, and deserve no credit; we have only done our duty' " (Luke 17:10). Paul says the same: "All alike have sinned and are deprived of the divine splendor" (Romans 3:23; see also 11:32).

Even our best efforts to love God and others are never totally unselfish. We look for some return: gratitude, recognition, some reward — if not in this world, then at least in the next. Totally disinterested love does not exist this side of heaven.

The essence of the Gospel is the good news that *God himself has made good what is lacking in our imperfect attempts to love.* He has sent his Son, Jesus, to love *for* us; to do, on our behalf, as representatives of all humankind, what we could never do for ourselves. Jesus, moreover, has accepted the sentence of condemnation which we deserve because of our lack of love. Jesus, though sinless, hangs on the cross in our place (see 2 Corinthians 5:21). He tells us in today's Gospel that he is the good shepherd who freely lays down his life for his foolish wandering sheep.

Our part is to *accept* what God offers us through his Son. This acceptance the New Testament calls "faith." And without faith in this sense we cannot be saved. The same Scriptures that tell us we cannot be saved without *love* also tell us we cannot be saved without *faith.* The seeming contradiction between those two statements disappears when we realize that love and faith are like two sides of the same coin. Both are ways in which we break out of the closed circle of our self-centeredness. *Love* directs us to the service of others, to the point of self-forgetfulness. *Faith* admits that even our best efforts to serve are tainted by egotism. Hence faith reaches out in *trust* to Him who, on our behalf, has made up for our imperfect love, and has borne for us the punishment for failing to love as we should.

This is the basis for Peter's claim that "there is no salvation in anyone else" than in Jesus Christ. If there is salvation for anyone, it is only because of Jesus, the good shepherd, whose care for the sheep is totally disinterested; who loves us, his foolish sheep, enough to lay down his life for us.

Jesus died as he had lived: for others. Jesus is "the man for others." There is a solidarity between Jesus Christ and the rest of humankind. We become *sharers* in this solidarity through our faith in Jesus Christ. Like him, we are called to be "people for others"; to lay down *our* lives for our sisters and brothers, as Jesus laid down *his* life for *us*.

Our call — and our privilege — is the same as that given to Simon of Cyrene. As he helped Jesus carry the cross to Calvary, so we are privileged to carry the same cross through history. The faithfulness with which we do so affects the quality of life in our generation, and so the fate of millions who may never accept Christ or his teaching.

We who have become Catholic Christians in baptism are called to supply in our generation a measure of the selfless love we see in Jesus Christ. We are called to trusting faith in him who alone was capable of perfect love — that love without which human life disintegrates into a ghastly confusion of selfish rivalries, and bloody wars.

No one has said it better than St. John, in our second reading.

> How great is the love that the Father has shown to us! We were called God's children, and such we are; and the reason

why the godless world does not recognize us is that it has not known him. Here and now, dear friends, we are God's children; what we shall be has not yet been disclosed, but we know that when it is disclosed we shall be like him, because we shall see him as he is.

John 15:1-8

"I AM THE TRUE VINE."

- *To show the implications, for faith and life, of Jesus' teaching about the vine and the branches.*

Over the entrance to the Jerusalem Temple in Jesus' day was a gilded relief of a vine with grape clusters as tall as a man. It symbolized God's people. He had delivered them, under Moses, from slavery in Egypt. God had "planted" his people, one of the psalms said, in the land they now called their own, as a farmer plants a vine (Psalm 80:8-16).

With infinite patience God had tended and cared for his planting. Too often he had been disappointed. The vine failed to yield the fruit God hoped for. As the prophet Isaiah said: "He looked for it to yield grapes, but it yielded wild grapes" (5:2c). Yet God continued to hope for an abundant harvest. Isaiah said that this harvest, when it came, would be a sign of the messianic age, when God's anointed servant would visit his people. "On that day . . . Israel shall bud and blossom, and they shall fill the whole earth with fruit" (27:2, 6).

Only when we know this rich symbolism can we appreciate the full force of Jesus' words in today's Gospel. It was the night before his death. Jesus had celebrated the Last Supper with his closest friends. One of them had left the table to betray the Master. "Arise, let us go forth," Jesus said at the meal's conclusion (John 14:31). The words "I am the true vine" follow at once.

Some Bible scholars suggest that Jesus may have spoken

these words as he crossed the Temple courtyard with his eleven still-faithful friends. It was Passover time, so there would have been, as always at that festival, a full moon. The golden vine over the Temple door would have been clearly visible, glowing in the soft light. It is even possible that Jesus pointed first to the vine and then to himself as he said: "I am the *true* vine." These words, and those that follow, make three statements:

- about Jesus himself;
- about his followers;
- and about his Father.

In calling himself the true vine, Jesus implied a contrast. God's people had not been true. By their unfaithfulness they had failed to produce the harvest God looked for. Jesus *had* been true. His death the next day would be Jesus' final act of faithful obedience to his Father's will. Even now, the little band of friends accompanying him were the firstfruits of the harvest that God looked for when he sent his Son into the world.

> My Father has been glorified in your bearing much fruit and becoming my disciples.

Jesus' words were also a statement about his followers. They too must bear fruit. A condition of their doing so was that they remain united to him and seek to do his will.

> Live on in me, as I do in you. No more than a branch can bear fruit of itself apart from the vine, can you bear fruit apart from me.

The person who remains united with him, Jesus said, "will produce abundantly." He went further still:

> If you live in me, and my words stay part of you, you may ask
> what you will — it will be done for you.

Jesus was *not* saying that his followers had some kind of supernatural power to get anything they wanted. He was saying that if we are truly united to him in heart, mind and will, our requests would always be in harmony with what he wants. Hence the Father would always be able to grant these requests.

Finally, there is Jesus' statement about his Father. He is the vinegrower who cares for the branches in two ways: by burning the unfruitful ones, and by pruning those that bear fruit. Jesus' words about the vinegrower cutting away and burning the unfruitful branches were an implied reference to Judas, who was even then betraying the Lord. Judas is the "withered rejected branch, picked up to be thrown in the fire and burnt." In the parable of the wheat and the weeds, Jesus warned that there might be others as well (see Matthew 13:30).

The vinegrower's treatment of the fruitful branches seems at first sight harsh: "He trims [them] clean to increase their yield." The image is that of a gardener pinching off the new green shoots on a vine, so that all the growth can be concentrated in the few early-blooming branches which the gardener has selected to bear fruit.

When we experience reverses, injustice or suffering, we naturally ask: "Why me? What have I done to deserve all this?" Such questions are unanswerable. Jesus' words in today's Gospel do not answer such questions. Rather they are a challenge: to view setbacks and suffering as *opportunities to grow.*

That was how Paul dealt with suffering. He writes in his second letter to the Corinthians about a trial that he called

far too heavy for us to bear, so heavy that we even despaired of life. Indeed we felt in our hearts that we had received a death sentence.

Yet Paul viewed this suffering as a challenge:

This was meant to teach us not to place reliance on ourselves, but on God who raises the dead.

(2 Corinthians 1:8f)

Where did Paul get the inner vision and strength to rise above suffering in this way? From his heavenly Father and ours, whom Jesus in today's Gospel calls "the vinegrower."

Jesus invites us to do the same: to submit to the vinegrower's pruning, and so to glorify him by producing abundant fruit.

Sixth Sunday of Easter

John 15:9-17

"THAT MY JOY MAY BE YOURS."

• *To show the hearers the way to Christian joy.*

Was Jesus a joyful person? Or was he sad and serious? The Gospels show that he was both: serious, even sad, when that was appropriate; yet also so filled with joy that he could say, in today's Gospel: "All this I tell you *that my joy may be yours.*"

What about ourselves? Are *we* joyful people? Even a casual glance at the faces in church on Sunday morning suggests very strongly that many of us, at least, are not particularly joyful. Many Catholics experience their religion as dreary, boring and joyless. Why?

One reason is the importance we give to fulfilling our Sunday obligation. It *is* important. Obligations are necessary in every life. They are a kind of safety net. There are many times in life when we just don't feel like doing what we should do. Obligations help us through such times. If we only prayed or attended Mass when we felt like it, how deep and strong would our faith be? When faithfulness to private prayer and public worship is *costly*, because it goes against our natural inclinations, we are offering God something that is especially pleasing to him. Such costly offerings strengthen our faith and deepen faith.

At the same time, a religion that never gets beyond the fulfillment of a list of minimum obligations is always joyless. Religious practice of that kind is like the attitude of children

91

who ask, whenever they are asked to do something they don't like: "Do I *have* to?" The all too familiar tone of voice in which young people ask that question shows that it is a childish question, not an adult one. People who go through life asking, "Do I have to?" are people without joy. No wonder that Catholics who are always asking that question about their religion find it a burden, rather than a source of joy.

What is the solution? One that is often proposed is that we reduce the list of obligations, on the ground that people today will not sacrifice as much as their parents and grandparents did. That is no solution at all. Whenever there has been a resurgence of joy among the followers of Jesus Christ, it has never come through less devotion and sacrifice, but always through more. We see this fundamental law of Church life at work today precisely in those parts of the world where the Church is most vital and alive: not in countries where practice of the faith is easy, but where it is *difficult.*

What do we Catholics in this comfortable and prosperous land know, for instance, about the sacrifices necessary to be loyal to Jesus Christ and his Church in a country like Poland, where being known as a practicing Catholic can exclude people from higher education and a good job? Or what do we know of the devotion of masses of African Catholics, who often travel for miles on foot to Mass and, once there, celebrate the liturgy with an enthusiasm and joy that we associate with sporting events, but never with Mass?

Catholics who never get beyond fulfilling a list of minimum obligations are really trying, whether they realize it or not, to keep God on the fringe of their lives. He seems less threatening at a distance. In fact, precisely the opposite is true. As long as we keep God on the fringe of our lives, he will always be a threat to us. He will always be trying to move into the center. God stops being a threat only when he is *already* at the center of our lives!

This was where God was in Jesus' life. He tells his disciples in today's Gospel:

"I have kept my Father's commandments, and live in his love." God was never on the fringe of Jesus' life. He was always at the center. That is what "living in the Father's love" means. A relationship of love is never based upon fulfilling minimum obligations. If we truly love someone, we never ask how little we can do for that person, but how *much*. People in love are constantly looking for fresh ways to show their love to one another by increasing each other's joy.

Jesus lived such a relationship of love throughout his entire life. He put God, his Father, at the *center* of his life. Jesus never asked: "Do I *have* to?" The obligations imposed on Jesus by his religion were far more onerous than the obligations we Catholics have today. Yet Jesus never worried, as so many of us do, about fulfilling his obligations. Jesus fulfilled all his obligations automatically, because he was constantly asking not how *little* he could do for God, but how much.

It was because God was at the *center* of his life, all the time, that Jesus could say in today's Gospel:

"All this I tell you that my joy may be yours."

That is what Jesus Christ wants for every one of us: not less joy, but more: "that my joy may be yours, and your joy may be *complete*."

Do you want that joy in *your* life? It is yours for the taking. To find the joy of which Jesus speaks in today's Gospel, you need to do just one thing. You must begin to fall in love with Jesus Christ. Does that sound difficult? It would be im-

93

possibly difficult, save for one crucial fact. The One who invites you to fall in love with him — that his joy may be yours, and that your joy may be complete — is *already* in love with you.

"There is no greater love than this," Jesus tells us in today's Gospel. "To lay down one's life for one's friends."

That is what Jesus Christ has already done — for you.

Ascension Thursday

Acts 1:1-11; Ephesians 1:17-23; Mark 16:15-20

"SEATED AT GOD'S RIGHT HAND."

• *To show how the Ascension inaugurates the age of the Church, with its missionary task that involves all the baptized.*

Was Jesus' ascension a conclusion or a beginning? Probably any one of us would answer: "A conclusion." For Mark, however, Jesus' ascension was clearly a *beginning*.

> The Lord continued to work with them throughout and confirm the message through the signs which accompanied them.

These final words in today's Gospel look not backward, but forward. For Mark, indeed for all the New Testament writers, Jesus' ascension inaugurated a new age: the age of the Church, in which we live. In and through the Church Jesus continues through history the work he began during his earthly life. To do so he wants to work through every one of us who in baptism has become a member of his Church.

The New Testament conviction that Jesus' ascension inaugurated a new age survives even in our post-Christian and secular age. It is reflected in the way we number the years. We designate the years before the birth of Christ "B.C." — before Christ. The years since then are called not "after Christ," but "A.D. — anno Domini," which is Latin for "in the year of the Lord." These are the years that belong to him who is Lord of history. This is the final age, at the end of which Jesus Christ will come again: not in weakness and obscurity, as he came at Bethlehem; but in power and glory. This is the meaning of the angels' message that closed our first reading:

> This Jesus who has been taken from you will return, just as you saw him go up into the heavens.

That is picture language, of course: poetic imagery to suggest something beyond the power of language to describe literally. And the Gospel is using picture language when it says that Jesus is seated "at God's right hand." This does not mean that Jesus is in a certain place, but that he exercises a certain *function*. He is our *prophet*, our *priest*, and our *king*.

A *prophet* is not necessarily someone who predicts the future, but rather a person who speaks for God. Jesus, who spoke for God in his earthly life, continues this prophetic utterance through his holy word: written in Scripture, proclaimed by his Church.

Jesus is our *priest* because it is through him that we approach the Father. We conclude every prayer "through Jesus Christ," in the power of his Holy Spirit.

Today's second reading speaks of Jesus as *king* when it says, again using picture language, that God

> has put all things under Christ's feet and has made him thus exalted, head of the church, which is his body: the fullness of him who fills the universe in all its parts.

The Church is the sphere where Christ's kingly rule is acknowledged. The world in which the Church lives today rejects its true king, and suffers in consequence the turmoil, chaos, and anguish of which we see the daily evidence in our newspapers and on the television news. The task of the Church, which means the task of every one of us who makes up the Church, is to *expand* the sphere in which Christ's rule is acknowledged. We do so not so much by words (for words are cheap), as by the contagious force of our example.

Jesus commands us, as he commanded that little band of eleven men on a Galilean hillside two thousand years ago, to "Go into the whole world and proclaim the good news to all creation." In the measure in which we try faithfully to fulfill this command, Jesus continues to do for us what he did for them: "to confirm the message through signs." In the pre-scientific world of the first century, there were signs appropriate to that age: the power to expel demons, to speak other languages and immunity to deadly influences and disease. Today's signs are different: the worldwide inspiration of a Mother Teresa, the serene and cheerful faith of a Pope John XXIII, the heroism of countless martyrs in this bloodiest of all centuries to date.

The greatest of all today's signs, however, is simply this: that despite so much failure, so many frustrations, and so many defeats in the struggle to fulfill Christ's missionary command, nevertheless after twenty centuries so many are still trying.

Seventh Sunday of Easter

John 17:11-19

IN THE WORLD, NOT OF THE WORLD.

• *To show the implications of Jesus' high-priestly prayer: "Guard them from the evil one."*

Is there anyone here who has never known the satisfaction of a job well done? A woman beams with pride as she brings a favorite dish to the table. A man is happy as he contemplates the neat patterns left by the lawnmower on the grass he has just cut. A student rejoices when the term paper that has cost so much labor is finally finished on time. Yes, and preachers are happy when the sermon is ready on Friday, and Saturday can be used for other duties.

Jesus expresses this joy in today's Gospel. He knows that his life is drawing to its close. Yet even as he consecrates himself for his sacrificial death, Jesus can pray to his Father for his followers, "that they may share my joy completely."

How can Jesus speak of joy in the face of death? Because he knows he has completed the work he was sent into the world to accomplish. Satisfaction at the fulfillment of his life's work remained with Jesus to the end. "It is accomplished" were his final words on the cross (John 19:30).

Jesus' joy in today's Gospel is akin to the joy of the creative artist over the completion of a masterpiece. Jesus' joy comes from having brought the Church into being. The whole of today's Gospel is a prayer for the Church.

O Father most holy, protect them with your name which you have given me. . . . Guard them from the evil one. . . . As you

98

have sent me into the world, so I have sent them into the world.

Jesus sends *us* into the world just as he sent his first followers. Of us too he says, as he says of them:

"They are not of the world, any more than I am of the world." We are to influence and affect the world, without being dominated by it. We are to be the world's salt (see Matthew 5:13), and the world's yeast (13:33): elements which are quantitatively small, yet qualitatively make all the difference.

Fully aware how difficult it is to be the world's salt and yeast, Jesus prays to his Father:

I do not ask you to take them out of the world, but to guard them from the evil one.

Jesus gave this same prayer to us when he told us to pray: "Deliver us from evil."

The power of the evil one was something very real to Jesus. He experienced this power during his temptations in the wilderness. Though the details of those temptations seem bizarre, in their essentials they are not difficult to understand.

The suggestion that Jesus turn stones into bread was the temptation to use his divine powers for his own satisfaction. The suggestion that he throw himself down from the Temple was the temptation to challenge God to make good on his promise of supernatural protection after all normal precautions and prudence had been thrown to the winds. The suggestion that Jesus purchase a worldly kingdom by worshiping the evil one was the temptation to seek spiritual success by worldly means: to substitute a political kingdom of power and glory for the spiritual kingdom of love and service for the sake of which Jesus had been sent into the world.

Jesus prayed his Father to keep us "from the evil one" because he knew we would experience temptations very similar to his. We would be tempted to use God's gift of truth, love and grace for ourselves: for the sake of the warm, spiritual feelings they give us. In reality, however, God gives us his gifts to enable us to be *people for others*; to be salt and yeast — those small ingredients which are unnoticed, until they are missing!

Jesus knew how often we would be tempted to live imprudently and foolishly, trusting that God would look after us because of the prayers we said. That is the sin of presumption. It is presumption when students neglect their studies all semester, and then pray frantically for a miracle at exam time. It is presumption to damage with massive quantities of alcohol, nicotine, or junk food the wonderful bodies God has given us — and then expect miraculous deliverance when we succumb to disease or stress. Yes, and it is presumption when the Church seeks special privileges or protection from the state, or from the rich and powerful; and yet still expects to remain credible as the messenger and spokesman of him who was the friend of sinners, the outcast, the poor, and who had nowhere to lay his head (see Luke 9:58).

Jesus asked his heavenly Father to protect us from the evil one because he knew how often we would be tempted to think we could take moral shortcuts to accomplish good ends. Whenever we yield to that temptation we can be sure of one thing: *no* good will be accomplished. We succumb to this temptation whenever in individual life, or in the life of the

Church, we lie, or cheat, or steal, or take unfair advantage —
and then excuse these moral shortcuts by saying piously: "It
was all in a good cause."

Against all these things and many more like them Jesus
prays his Father in today's Gospel:

> I do not ask you to take them out of the world, but to guard
> them from the evil one.

Confident that the Father will answer this prayer, Jesus
asks also "that they may share my joy completely."

That is our opportunity, and our calling: to share the joy of
our divine Lord, and to share his joy completely. Jesus, before
all others, was in the world, yet not of the world; acting upon
the world, yet never subject to the world's sin, darkness and
evil. Jesus prays in today's Gospel:

> Holy Father, as you have sent me into the world, so I have sent
> them into the world.

We share in the sending and mission that God the Father
gave his Son Jesus. There can be no destiny higher than that,
no life more worth living. That, and nothing less than that, is
the destiny and the life which were given to us when, in baptism, we became sisters and brothers of him who laid down
his life for us, and who is alive forevermore.

Pentecost

Acts 2:1-11; John 20:19-23

"TONGUES AS OF FIRE."

• *To help the hearers understand the Pentecost event and its significance for our lives.*

Did anyone notice a seeming contradiction between the first reading and the Gospel? The first reading said that the Holy Spirit was given publicly on the Jewish feast of Pentecost. The Gospel told us that Jesus imparted the Holy Spirit privately on the evening of his resurrection. Which version is correct?

We cannot say. However interesting such a question may be for us, it would have had little interest, or even meaning, for the biblical writers. They were not primarily interested in the When and the Where of the events they described. They were far more interested in the Who. The creation stories in Genesis, for instance, tell us *who* made the world. For information about the When, Where, and How of creation we must consult not the Bible, but natural science.

If we ask *who* gave the Spirit, both of today's accounts agree. The Spirit is the gift of the risen Lord Jesus. This is explicit in the Gospel. And it is equally clear if we read our first reading, from chapter two of Acts, in the context of what has preceded it in chapter one. There the risen Lord Jesus commands his followers to wait at Jerusalem for his promised gift of the Spirit.

What — or better who — *is* the Holy Spirit? The Spirit is the love who binds together the Father and the Son. The Ger-

102

man Jesuit Alfred Delp, who gave his life for Jesus Christ on February 2, 1945, under the tyranny of Adolf Hitler, wrote with shackled hands in a prison cell as he awaited the execution:

> The Holy Spirit is God's passion for himself. Man must make contact with this passion, must play his part in completing the circuit. Then true love will reign again in the world and man will be capable of living to the full. The indwelling presence of God must take possession of our senses, draw us out of ourselves, in order that we may be capable of genuine assent and contact. God must ratify himself in us and through us; then we shall live as we should. Then the holy fire will again become the heart of the earth and remain so.
>
> (A. Delp, *Facing Death*)

Pentecost celebrates Jesus' gift of the "holy fire." As our first reading told us: "Tongues as of fire appeared which parted and came to rest on each of them." Fire has three properties: it *burns*, it *spreads*, and it *gives light.*

1. God is a consuming fire who *burns* all he touches. When God appeared to Moses, it was in a burning bush. The Letter to the Hebrews tells us: "It is a terrible thing to fall into the hands of the living God" (10:31). The realization that God is a burning fire explains why many people try to keep God at a distance. They crowd into the back pews of the church. They come to Mass late and hurry away early. They resist all efforts to involve them actively in worship. They prefer a liturgy performed by specialists: the "holy man" and his assistants at a distant altar. A liturgy that asks the active participation of all the worshipers makes people who fear the fire of God's love uncomfortable.

2. As fire burns, it *spreads*. "I have come to set fire to the

earth," Jesus says, "and how I wish it were already kindled" (Luke 12:49). That we are Catholic Christians in a continent undreamed of by anyone in Jerusalem on the first Pentecost is proof that the fire kindled then was not lit in vain. It is our task to pass the flame on to others, so that they may catch a spark from the fire of God's love burning within us. Christianity, it has been said, cannot be taught. It must be caught.

3. As it burns and spreads, fire *gives light*. We are called to be prisms of God's light, so that it may shine in a dark world. We cannot do so if our lives are darkened by sin. That is why, in the Gospel, Jesus connects the gift of his Spirit with the power to forgive sins. The inner quality of our lives is determining, right now, the brightness or the darkness of that part of the world in which God's providence has placed us. St. Paul tells us what this means in characteristically memorable words (Philippians 2:12-16).

> Work out your own salvation in fear and trembling; for it is God who works in you, inspiring both the will and the deed, for his chosen purpose. Do all you have to do without complaint or wrangling. Show yourselves guileless and above reproach, faultless children of God in a warped and crooked generation, in which you shine like stars in a dark world, and proffer the word of life.

None of us can do that, or even begin to do that, on our own. With joy, therefore, on this feast of Pentecost, we join the Church's unceasing prayer for the Spirit's gifts.

> Come down, O love divine, seek thou this soul of mine,
> And visit it with thine own ardor glowing;
> O Comforter, draw near, within my heart appear
> And kindle it, thy holy flame bestowing.

O let it freely burn, till earthly passions turn
To dust and ashes in its heat consuming;
And let thy glorious light shine ever on my sight,
And clothe me round, the while my path illuming.

Let holy charity mine outward vesture be,
And lowliness become mine inner clothing;
True lowliness of heart, which takes the humbler part,
And o'er its own shortcomings weeps with loathing.

And so the yearning strong, with which the soul will long,
Will far outpass the power of human telling;
For none can guess its grace, till he become the place
Wherein the Holy Spirit makes his dwelling.

(Bianco da Siena, d. 1434;
translated by R.F. Littledale, d. 1890)

Trinity Sunday

Deuteronomy 4:32-34, 39-40; Romans 8:14-17; Matthew 28:16-20

THE THREEFOLD EXPERIENCE OF GOD.

* *To elucidate the mystery of the Trinity by reference to our experience of prayer.*

Surveys reveal that far more people pray than ever attend church. In fact, there are probably few people who have never prayed at any time in their lives. Prayer is as natural as eating or sleeping, and almost as universal.

What are we doing when we pray? At the simplest level, we are trying to get in touch with God. Before we start, however, we already have some concept of God. This may have various sources. For Christians the primary source of our image of God is Jesus, the man who *is* God: completely human, as we are; yet also completely divine. Moreover, prayer does not really start with us at all. We could not even begin to pray if God had not already given us the desire to get in touch with him, and if he did not assist us as we try to do so.

The simple act of praying has a threefold pattern. First, God is the one we are trying to get in touch with when we pray. Second, we already have an idea or image of God before we pray, and its source is Jesus Christ. And third, it is God himself who gives us the desire to pray, and who helps us as we do so.

There is a similar threefold pattern in today's first reading. Moses speaks first of God's work in creation: "Ask now of the days of old . . . ever since God created man upon the earth." This Creator-God is no remote "Great Architect of the universe," however, who remains uninvolved in his handiwork. From all the nations of the earth, Moses says, God chose one to be especially his own. He made himself this people's Deliverer and Lawgiver. God brought his people out of Egypt "with his strong hand and outstretched arm . . . before your very eyes," Moses reminds them. And God gave his people the Ten Commandments atop Mt. Sinai with thunder and lightning, "speaking from the midst of the fire." Third, this Creator, who is also Deliverer and Lawgiver in one, looks for a *response* from his people: "You must keep his statutes and commandments . . . that you and your children after you may prosper."

In the second reading Paul calls this response "the spirit of adoption." He explains this as the ability to address the God who is both Creator and Deliverer as Father. The word Paul uses, Abba, was in his language the intimate word for father, the equivalent of our word "Daddy." The ability to address our Creator and Deliverer in that intimate way is not something we can attain of ourselves, Paul says. It is God's gift. "You have received a spirit of adoption through which we cry out, 'Abba!' (that is, 'Father')."

Paul's words reflect the same threefold pattern we saw in the first reading. First, there is God the Creator. Second, this Creator-God becomes his people's Deliverer and Lawgiver. Third, he himself enables them to respond to creation and deliverance with the obedient love of children, expressed in the intimate form of address: "Abba — Father."

This threefold pattern becomes explicit in Jesus' parting command to his apostles in today's Gospel.

Go, make disciples of all the nations. Baptize them in the name of the Father, and of the Son, and of the Holy Spirit.

Those words tell us that God who is one is also three. This is the doctrine of the Trinity.

Because the Trinity is called a mystery, people assume it can be understood only by learned experts. You could fill a library with the books that theologians have written about the Trinity.

Yet the simplest believer without any formal education *experiences* what those books are trying to say simply by turning to God in prayer. Even children, when they pray, have the threefold experience of God with which we began.

Take a little girl kneeling by her bedside at night. Before she begins to pray, God *is*. Second, the child has some idea of this God before kneeling down. This is based on what she knows of Jesus Christ. And third, the One who inspires the child to pray, and helps her to do so, is God himself. The child is *experiencing* Father, Son and Holy Spirit even though she may never have heard those terms, or may be too young to understand them.

On another level, however, the doctrine of the Trinity *is* a mystery. This does not mean that only people with unusual education or learning can understand God. No, God is a mystery in quite another sense. All we can know of God is only a fraction of the full truth about him. The language of the greatest poets, and the ideas of the most learned theologians and philosophers, are always far too small to capture God's richness, depth and majesty. We come closest to penetrating God's mystery not through study and learning, but through *love*: not just a warm *feeling*, but an attitude of the *will* that takes us out of ourselves and impels us to active service of God and others.

As an anonymous ancient Catholic writer has said: "By love

God may be caught and held; by thinking never" (*The Cloud of Unknowing*). To which we may add the words of St. John Vianney, the Curé or parish priest of Ars in France in the first part of the last century:

"In the heart that loves God it is always springtime."

Corpus Christi

Hebrews 9:11-15; Mark 14:12-16; 22-26

THE EUCHARIST AS MEAL, SACRIFICE, AND COVENANT.

* *To enhance the quality of worship by helping the hearers better understand three essential aspects of the Eucharist.*

Most of today's Catholics over thirty can still remember "the old Mass." The priest prayed in Latin, with his back to us most of the time. The central part of the Mass, the consecration, consisted of a long silence, punctuated only by the rattling of rosaries and the rustling of pages, as people with Latin-English missals tried to follow the action at the often distant altar.

In the midst of this silence, however, there was a dramatic climax, heralded by the ringing of a bell. Suddenly the church was hushed. Everyone's eyes were riveted on the priest's back, as he slowly raised above his head the host which he had just consecrated. A moment later we saw him elevate the chalice.

Children in Catholic schools were taught the words of consecration, which the priest whispered just before the elevation of the host and chalice: "This is my body . . . This is my blood." In high school, or at least in college theology courses, students studied the doctrine of transubstantiation: theologians' attempt to explain how Christ's body and blood are present on the altar under the outward forms of bread and wine.

The reason for this great emphasis of consecration and the presence of Christ's body and blood in the old Mass is rooted

110

in history. Since the Protestant Reformation of the sixteenth century many Christians have interpreted these truths in ways that Catholics cannot accept. Some Protestants, for instance, say that Jesus' words at the Last Supper should be understood in a purely symbolic sense: "This *means* or *signifies* my body."

Actually, Jesus said more than merely, "This is my body," and "This is my blood." He embedded each of those statements in a *command*: "Take this, all of you, and eat it. . . . Take this, all of you, and drink from it." Those commands were always part of the consecration even in the old Mass. They show that the Eucharist is a *meal*. The important thing about the consecration is not merely that Jesus comes to be *present* on the altar, but that he is present *as food*. Just as bread exists not merely for its own sake, but to be eaten, and as wine exists to be drunk, so Jesus offers us his body and blood in the Eucharist as our spiritual food and drink.

The Eucharist is a meal — but a special kind of meal. It is a *sacrificial* meal. At every Mass we repeat not only Jesus' statement over the cup, "This is my blood," but the words he immediately added: "It will be shed for you and for all, so that sins may be forgiven." For the first-century Jew, Jesus, the shedding of blood symbolized the offering of a life. Jesus laid down his life for us on Calvary, offering his Father a perfect, unblemished sacrifice for the sins of all humankind in all ages, our own sins included.

The new Eucharistic Prayers given to us by the Church in 1969 emphasize this sacrificial aspect of the Eucharist by adding to the words "This is my body" the phrase "which will be given up for you." At the time these words were introduced they seemed like an innovation. In reality they revived a tra-

111

dition from the first Christian generation, a tradition recorded in the New Testament (see Luke 22:19f; 1 Corinthians 11:24).

Our second reading said that Jesus' sacrifice on Calvary was offered "once for all." There is no repetition of Jesus' sacrifice in the Mass. Rather it is *sacramentally commemorated.* This means that in the unseen, spiritual realm Jesus' sacrifice on Calvary becomes, for us, *a living, present reality.* This aspect of the Mass is expressed in our third Eucharistic Acclamation, based on some words of St. Paul: "When we eat this bread, and drink this cup, we proclaim your death, Lord Jesus, until you come in glory." (See 1 Corinthians 11:26.)

Finally, this sacrificial meal is also a *covenant.* At every Mass we repeat Jesus' words: "This is the cup of my blood, the blood of the new and everlasting covenant." A covenant is a solemn pact or agreement that unites those who make the covenant. When, in obedience to Jesus' command at the Last Supper, we "do this" with the bread and the wine — sharing the one loaf, and drinking from the one cup — we are united in fellowship to the Father, in the love of his Son, who is present in the Eucharist in and through the power of his Holy Spirit. United in this way with Father, Son, and Holy Spirit, we are also joined in fellowship with all other sharers in this sacrificial meal and covenant.

Another way of stating this is to say that it is the Eucharist that *makes us Church*; for the Church is the fellowship of those who are united with God, and with one another. The Mass is not a form of private prayer — the soul alone with God. It is the common banquet of all God's people. When we exchange a greeting of peace before approaching the Lord's table, this is not an intrusion on our personal prayer. It is the acting out of one of the Eucharist's most essential aspects.

Here at the Eucharist Jesus nourishes us with his body and blood. Here we are present spiritually but truly in the Upper Room, and at Calvary. Here all the benefits of Jesus' one, unrepeatable sacrifice become available to us. Here we become sharers, through this sacrificial meal, in his "eternal covenant" which unites us with God, and with one another.

So much drama, so much wonder, so much spiritual treasure — and how seldom we realize it, and truly *worship*!

Second Sunday of the Year

John 1:35-42

"WHAT ARE YOU LOOKING FOR?"

- *To challenge the hearers to deeper conversion.*

"What are you looking for?" This question is Jesus' first recorded utterance in this Gospel according to John. Andrew
and his unnamed friend are not really certain *what* they are
looking for. They may have been following Jesus out of mere
curiosity. Challenged to say what they are looking for, they
counter with a question of their own: "Where do you stay?"
Jesus' response is hardly less challenging than his original
question: "Come and see."

In accepting this invitation, Andrew and his friend pass
from curiosity to discipleship. "Disciple" means a follower or
a learner. We read that "they stayed with [Jesus] that day."
The added information, that it was four in the afternoon, is
significant. The Jewish day begins not at midnight or dawn,
but in the late afternoon. Some scripture scholars think that
Andrew and his friend may have come to Jesus at four on a
Friday afternoon. That was the beginning of the Sabbath,
when all unnecessary movement and work were forbidden. In
this case these two new disciples of Jesus would have had to
stay with him not merely overnight, but the whole of the following Saturday as well.

What they said and did on that Sabbath, we do not learn. It
is clear, however, that those twenty-four hours in Jesus' company changed the lives of Andrew and his friend. For as soon
as the Sabbath restrictions are past, Andrew hurries to find

114

his brother Simon and give him momentous, almost unbelievable news: "We have found the Messiah!"

To encounter the anointed servant of the Lord, foretold by all the prophets, was the hope of every devout Jew. Yet who dared to expect the fulfillment of this hope? That seemed about as likely as our own chances of winning one of those hundred thousand dollar dream houses promised to the grand prize winner of the junk mail sweepstakes that flutter unbidden into our mailboxes every so often.

In accepting Jesus' invitation to "come and see," Andrew and his friend passed from curiosity to discipleship. In carrying the unbelievable news of his new Master's true identity to his brother Simon, Andrew moves from disciple to apostle. For "apostle" means "one who is sent"; a messenger, even an ambassador.

It is not difficult to imagine the excitement with which Andrew imparted his momentous message to his brother Simon. I have compared it to the excitement one of us would feel at winning one of today's mail-order sweepstakes. Jesus would use a similar comparison. The kingdom of heaven, he said once, was like a man finding buried treasure in a field; or like a merchant discovering a pearl so perfect that he gladly gave all he owned in order to possess it (see Matthew 13:44-46).

Into this deceptively simple incident the gospel writer has compressed a process which, for most people, takes far longer than the twenty-four hours recorded here. It is the process of moving from curiosity about Jesus Christ to discipleship; to becoming his apostle, or messenger, to others.

The process began, for Andrew and his friend, with Jesus' challenging question: "What are you looking for?" What are *you* looking for? Why have you come here today? Is it simply

115

to fulfill a legal obligation? What are you looking for in your *life*? Is it "the good life" advertised in glorious technicolor in the magazines and on the TV screens? Have you found the pursuit of that kind of happiness satisfying, and fulfilling? Or is it your experience that the good life, as defined by our contemporary hucksters, is not all it's made out to be? Is there still an emptiness inside you that you cannot fill, and longings that you cannot satisfy, try as you may?

What *are* you looking for? You may not know it, but at bottom you are looking for *love*. You want a love that will not let you go, that will not let you down. You yearn for a love that will not cheat or deceive or frustrate you; a love that will fulfill the deepest longings of your heart, your mind, your soul. *That* is what you are looking for. That is what I am looking for — what every one of us is looking for.

Perhaps you have grown weary with looking and think the search is hopeless. You are wrong. There *is* someone who can satisfy those deep longings within you. His name is Jesus Christ. Now, in this hour, he is challenging you with the same question he put to Andrew and his friend: "What are you looking for?" He is inviting you to come and stay with him. When you accept that invitation you pass from curiosity to discipleship. You become Jesus' friend, his follower, his disciple.

That is wonderful. That is beautiful. But it is not the end. Jesus Christ wants you to become his friend, his disciple, his follower, so that he can make you his *apostle*: his messenger and ambassador to carry the all-consuming love which he offers you to those to whom he sends you: his sisters and brothers — and yours too.

Third Sunday of the Year

1 Corinthians 7:29-31; Mark 1:14-20

"THE WORLD AS WE KNOW IT IS PASSING AWAY."

* *To explain Christian detachment and encourage the hearers to practice it.*

A word that was newly coined in the '60s and came into common use in the '70s is "dropout." Most of us know, or at least know of, someone who is a dropout. Probably the person is young. He or she has adopted a lifestyle which offends, and may deeply pain, the young person's parents: a way of living that proclaims complete disinterest in "the good life" as it is generally understood in our society today.

What is this "good life"? A rough description goes something like this: a nice house in the suburbs with a thirty-year mortgage, a happy marriage, two or three children, a dog and a recreational vehicle, a boat or a vacation cabin at a lake or the seashore.

The dropouts in our society are saying: "We don't want your 'good life' even if it's free." This protest can take various forms. It may mean living with a lover without marrying. Other dropouts put as much distance as possible between themselves and their families. Still others join some bizarre religious sect.

It is easy to criticize the dropouts and to point out the shortsightedness of their choices. We make it too easy for ourselves, however, if we simply criticize and condemn. The dropout is calling into question our society's fundamental values.

117

Paul is doing the same when he writes, in today's second reading: "The world as we know it is passing away." Paul recommends a "countercultural" way of living characterized by the phrase: "as if not." Married people, Paul says, should live as if they were not married; those who weep, as if they were not weeping and those who rejoice, as if they were not rejoicing; those involved in worldly business as if they were uninvolved.

Paul's reason for telling people to live "as if not" was his conviction that "the time is short." Paul believed that the end of the world and the return of Jesus Christ in glory were imminent. Hence there was not much point getting too involved in worldly affairs, which would be of short duration.

We no longer have Paul's confidence about an imminent return of Jesus Christ. As we approach the year 2000, however, we are sure to be bombarded with self-confident prophecies of the Second Coming. Indeed, if you have been watching some of the Sunday religious programming on television, you will be aware that the bombardment has already begun. Next time you hear someone who claims to know when the world will end, recall the words of Jesus Christ: "About that day and that hour no one knows, not even the angels in heaven, not even the Son; but only the Father" (Mark 13:32).

Paul may have been mistaken about the *date* of Christ's return. He was *right*, however, in saying that we are living in *the last age*. The world as we know it *is* passing away. The values of this world — the house in the suburbs, the happy marriage, children, dog, and recreational facilities — are real values. They are not the highest values, however, and certainly they are not ultimate values. To this extent the dropouts, who reject these things, are right.

118

Jesus himself warned against paying too much attention to the values of this world.

> Do not ask anxiously, What are we to eat? What are we to drink? What shall we wear? All these things are for heathen to run after, not for you.

The word translated "heathen" there means people without faith, whose vision is limited to the here and now. Jesus challenges us to *expand* our vision. "Set your mind on God's kingdom and his justice before everything else, and all the rest will come to you as well" (Matthew 6:31-33).

Where the dropouts are *wrong* is in assuming that the "good life" that they reject is of *no* value. The good things of this world are real gifts from our Creator. They are meant to be enjoyed, to enrich life, to be used for God's glory. They *cease* to be good, however, when they are no longer our servants and become our masters. Then they lose the power to make us happy. They begin instead to make us *un*happy, to fret and worry and be dissatisfied.

We who in baptism have been made brothers and sisters of Jesus Christ are called to live in God's world always conscious that "the world as we know it is passing away." Jesus summons some people to do this in a radical way. The disciples in today's Gospel received such a call. At Jesus' command "they immediately abandoned their nets and became his followers."

Most people, however, are called not to *abandonment* but to *detachment*. That is the "as if not" attitude recommended by Paul: using and enjoying the good things of this world — good human relationships and possessions; yet not allowing any of these things or people to *dominate* us or *possess* us.

Detachment is one of those things that can seldom be

pursued directly, however. We develop detachment quietly, even secretly, in the measure in which we become increasingly *attached* to Jesus Christ. That is why we are here: to be caught up, held fast, and kept safe by Christ's love — the love that will never let us go.

Fourth Sunday of the Year

1 Corinthians 7:32-35

MARRIAGE AND CELIBACY.

• *To explain Catholic teaching about marriage and celibacy, as a help especially to the many hearers who are not presently married.*

Why don't Catholic priests marry? Wouldn't priests be better able to help people with marriage problems if they *were* married? It used to be only non-Catholics who asked such questions. Today many Catholics ask them as well. Today's second reading gives us a good reason to consider these questions. Paul contended in that reading that unmarried people were more single-minded in serving God than the married.

> The unmarried man is busy with the Lord's affairs . . . but the married man is busy with this world's demands.

Is that really true?

To answer that question we need to know the situation in which Paul was writing. He was addressing people who considered marriage the only healthy, normal way of living. To such people Paul said, in effect: "Think again. The single life, especially when embraced for love of God, has unique advantages."

Our world is very different from Paul's. Yet today, as then, most people assume that everyone ought to be married. How often unmarried people in their mid-twenties and upwards have to answer the question: "When are you going to get married?" The assumption behind that question is that a neces-

121

sary ingredient of human happiness is an active sex life. This view is mistaken. What is necessary for happiness is not sex, but *love*. There is not a shred of evidence that this must always be directly sexual love, though for most adults that may be a normal way of expressing and experiencing love, at least during some part of their mature years.

When people ask, "Why celibacy?" one answer is: because of the witness celibate people give to a truth too often forgotten today, and even denied: that the single life is a *good* life; that it can be a *happy* life. It is estimated that roughly a third of the adult population in our society is not presently married. It is a grave disservice to these people to allow them to regard themselves as unfortunate and unfulfilled. To those of you who are not married, or no longer married, the Catholic Church, by honoring celibacy, proclaims the good news: "Your life can be happy, fulfilled, meaningful. As long as there is *love* in your life — love of God, love of others — you lack nothing necessary. You can hold your head high."

Honoring celibacy, however, is very different from *dishonoring* marriage. Let's face it. There are still some Catholics, including a few priests, who have the sneaking suspicion that there is something second-rate about marriage. Authentic Catholic teaching is that marriage, like celibacy, is *a high good*. Our sexuality is one of God's most beautiful gifts to us. The trouble with today's liberated sexuality is not that it allows people too much fun, but that it takes away wonder and reverence from one of God's holiest gifts by making it a purely bodily function hardly distinguishable from the coupling of animals. But what about Paul's claim that single people are more single-minded in serving God than the married? We must remember that Paul was writing to people who saw in celibacy nothing good at all. Hence he points out an *advantage* of the consecrated single life: freedom from family responsibilities makes it possible to serve God and others in ways not open to those who are married.

Moreover Paul was writing a *letter*. Had he been composing a balanced *treatise*, he would probably have mentioned a unique *danger* in the single life: the constant temptation to please not the Lord, but one's self; to sink from consecrated celibacy into a selfish bachelor existence.

Even when we have said all this, however, we are still left with the question: Why celibacy? Isn't it a terrible waste? People who ask those questions often raise similar questions about marriage. Why be faithful, they want to know, to a promise made years ago in completely different circumstances; after the one to whom the promise was made has changed, and I have changed too; when love has grown cold, and I see a chance for happiness with someone else who is now more attractive to me than my spouse?

To all such questions, whether directed at celibacy, or at faithfulness in marriage, a satisfactory answer is possible only within the context of *faith*. Faith involves the ability to see that there are values beyond the values of this world, values rooted in that unseen spiritual world which is all round us: the world of the saints, the angels, our beloved dead — the world of God.

So when people ask "Why celibacy?" or "Why faithfulness in marriage?" we reply: Without faith no justification is possible. *With* faith no justification is necessary. All of us, then, married or single, need to pray always: "Lord, I believe. Help my unbelief."

Fifth Sunday of the Year

Job 7:1-4, 6-7; Mark 1:29-39

THE HEALING POWER OF CHRIST CRUCIFIED.

• *To help the hearers be open to the healing power of Christ, God's personal Word to us.*

Have you ever suffered from sleeplessness? If so, you will be able to sympathize with Job, complaining in today's first reading:

> Troubled nights have been told off for me. If in bed I say, "When shall I arise?" then the night drags on; I am filled with restlessness until dawn.

The people who thronged around Jesus suffered from ailments far worse than insomnia. According to the prescientific ideas of the day their ills were due to demons. Today's Gospel describes a typical scene.

> After sunset, as evening drew on, they brought [to Jesus] all who were ill and those possessed by demons. Before long the whole town gathered outside the door.

Jesus was constantly surrounded by crowds like that. They flocked to him because they had heard of his miraculous healings. They regarded Jesus as a wonder-worker.

Jesus was clearly unhappy with this role. This is evident at two points in today's Gospel. First, when Simon Peter tried to persuade Jesus to resume his work of healing the next morning, Jesus refused. He explained that his real task was not to heal, but to preach.

Let us move on to the neighboring villages so that I may proclaim the good news there also. That is what I have come to do.

A second sign of Jesus' unhappiness with the role of wonder-working is that he did not allow the demons to speak, "because they knew him." In Mark's Gospel the first person who is permitted to proclaim Jesus' true identity is the Roman officer in charge at Calvary. He saw Jesus not as a wonder-worker, but as a common criminal suffering a death which seems to us ghastly in its cruelty, but which, to this hardened soldier, was routine. Yet something in *this* criminal's bearing moved that nameless Roman centurion to say, following Jesus' death: "Truly this man was the son of God" (Mark 15:39).

How do *you* regard Jesus Christ? Do you see him as a wonder-worker? Someone with supernatural powers who offers you a quick fix, who can get you out of a jam and rescue you when you are in beyond your depth?

Here in the Eucharist we encounter Jesus Christ. He does not come to us, however, as a wonder-worker with a quick solution to all our problems. We encounter him as the centurion encountered him: crucified in weakness.

Yet we also encounter Christ as the centurion did not. He comes to us as the risen Lord. He has not come back from death to the life he left, like his friend Lazarus. Jesus was raised from his tomb to a *new* life: one no longer subject to death — eternal life *beyond* death.

This crucified-and-risen Lord comes to us here in the Eucharist not with a quick fix, but with the healing power of God's life-giving word. Indeed Jesus *is* God's Word: his living, personal communication to us. There is healing power in this crucified and risen Lord who is God's Word. Jesus heals us by telling us that God loves us; by assuring us that God is always close to us, no matter how far we may stray from him. There is healing in Jesus' assurance that God accepts us in love as we are; that he does not wait for us to become the ideal people we would like to be before giving us his love.

Jesus who is God's personal Word tells us that God loves us enough to exchange his divine power for weakness. We see this at Bethlehem, where Jesus was weak and vulnerable as all babies are. We see it at Calvary, where Jesus accepted the weakness and final defeat of crucifixion.

Jesus is so much more than a mere wonder-worker. He invites us to open ourselves to the healing power of his word: the word he came to proclaim, the Word he himself *is*, in his own person. As we listen to him who is God's Word, God's personal message of life and hope, Jesus invites us to be filled with a sense of awe and wonder at the greatness of God's undeserved love for us. He invites us to respond to that love with a love of our own — by making him the center of our lives.

Sixth Sunday of the Year

Leviticus 13:1-2, 44-46; Mark 1:40-45

HEALED, RESTORED, FORGIVEN.

- *To bring home to the hearers the healing power of God's unconditioned love.*

To be shunned by someone you love is one of life's greatest hurts. It happens between friends, between lovers, between husband and wife. They quarrel, and afterwards avoid each other's company, or refuse to speak when they must be together. Most of us have been through experiences like that. We know how much it hurts to be shunned.

The leper who came to Jesus in today's Gospel was shunned by everyone except his fellow lepers. Leprosy was the dread scourge of the ancient world, worse than cancer today. Because the disease was thought to be highly contagious, the leper had to live apart. Since there was no cure for his illness, his situation was hopeless.

The leper in today's Gospel, however, had heard about a man named Jesus who could cure people, even those with incurable diseases like leprosy. With a hope born of despair he dared to violate the law we heard in the first reading that commanded lepers "to live apart." The leper threw himself at Jesus' feet, and begged for healing. "If you will, you can cure me."

Notice how Jesus reacts. He does not show revulsion. He is not afraid he will be contaminated. Jesus is "moved with pity." Though everyone else shuns the man, Jesus does not. Though the man's situation is hopeless, for Jesus it is not.

127

Though everyone else flees from the man in horror, Jesus does not. Instead Jesus does the unthinkable. He reaches out to *touch* the leper. At Jesus' word the man is cured. His life is changed in a single moment. He is restored to his friends and to society. He can lead a normal life again.

This simple story, set in a world so different from ours, has good news for us. It tells us that Jesus is the friend of the outcast, that he rejects no one who comes to him. Now, as then, Jesus' touch gives hope where there is no hope; restores people to fellowship with one another, and with God.

When we were little, our parents (if they were good parents) punished us when we were bad, and rewarded us when we were good. We grew up thinking God would do the same. If we want God to reward and bless us, we assume, we must first do something to *deserve* his blessing. Yet if we are honest every one of us has to admit that most of the time we are not deserving. Repeatedly we have *forfeited* any claim we might have on God for his blessing and reward. The logical conclusion is that our situation is hopeless — as hopeless as the leper's situation before he encountered Jesus Christ.

The good news of the Gospel is that our situation is *not* hopeless. God loves us *as we are right now*. He does not love us because we are good enough, for we are not. God loves us because *he* is so good that he *wants* to share his love and goodness with us.

For this good news to bear fruit in our lives, however, we need to do what the man in today's Gospel did. We must recognize the hopelessness of our situation and come to Jesus for healing. The leper needed no reminder of his hopelessness. The society which segregated and shunned him reminded him of it at every moment.

128

Many people, however, have difficulty recognizing the things in their lives that cry out for Jesus' healing touch, for forgiveness. They have worn a mask for so long that they can no longer see the real self behind the mask. If you are completely satisfied with your life as it is — with your character, your attitudes, your achievements — then the good news of the Gospel is, for you, no good news. Jesus cannot reach you with his healing power.

If, on the other hand, you are willing to come to Jesus Christ, as the leper did — if you will tell him how desperately you need him — then you too will experience his healing, and his forgiveness. You have only to come. Jesus is waiting for you.

Jesus sent the leper to the Jewish priest, as a sign that the man was restored to the holy fellowship of God's people and could join again in their worship. Those whom Jesus heals and forgives today he sends to their sisters and brothers to share with them the divine gifts of healing and forgiveness. How terrible to experience Jesus' healing and forgiveness and then to be, with others, hard-hearted, unforgiving: a talebearer, a gossip, tearing people down instead of building them up; a person who opens wounds instead of closing them, who destroys hope instead of sharing it!

The message of today's Gospel is simple. It is this. Jesus Christ gives hope where there is no hope. Jesus Christ cures the incurable, forgives the unforgivable. Jesus Christ welcomes outcasts and restores them to fellowship with God, and with God's holy people. Jesus Christ changes lives.

Jesus Christ can change *your* life. You have only to admit your need — and come.

Seventh Sunday of the Year

Isaiah 43:18-19, 21-22, 24b-25; Mark 2:1-12

THE MIRACLE OF FORGIVENESS.

* *To encourage contrition by showing the magnitude of God's gift of forgiveness.*

If you could start a chapter of your life over again, is there anything you would do differently? There can be few people here who would not answer "Yes" to that question. We know, however, that we can never go back in life. We can only go forward.

For those who find this universal law of life a burden, Jesus Christ has good news. Though life never allows us to go back, in going forward we need not drag behind us an ever lengthening tale of guilty mistakes. There is One who stands ready to lift this heavy burden from our shoulders. His name is Jesus Christ.

It was to free people from their burdens that Jesus Christ was born. For this he freely poured out his life's blood on the cross, "for you and for all, so that sins may be forgiven" — Jesus' words to his closest friends the night before he died. We repeat those words at every Eucharist when, obeying Jesus' command, we "do this" as a living memorial of his sacrificial death, which won forgiveness for us.

"My son, your sins are forgiven," Jesus says as he looks with tender love at the paralyzed man lying before him in today's Gospel. These words do not mean that sick people are being punished for sin. The words suggest, however, that Jesus had discerned in *this* particular man a spiritual burden that needed to be loosed before the man could be healed physically.

The onlookers are astonished to see the man rise and walk away unaided. "We have never seen anything like this," they exclaim. For the Gospel writer Mark, however, the true miracle is not the physical cure, but the spiritual healing of forgiveness.

Perhaps someone is thinking: "What is so miraculous about forgiveness? Don't people forgive each other every day?" Thank God, they do. Between our forgiveness and God's, however, there is this great difference. When *we* forgive, there is always a memory of the injury done, a skeleton in the closet. The wrong needs only to be repeated, or one like it, for the memory to be revived.

With God there is no skeleton in the closet. God's forgiveness is total. "Your sins I remember no more," God says in today's first reading. *That* is the miracle: that there can be, and is, a forgiveness so complete that not even the memory of the sin remains. Jesus brings us this total forgiveness. He is the representative and Son of the God who says in our first reading:

> You burdened me with your sins and wearied me with your crimes. But I wipe out your offenses, your sins *I remember no more.*

Jesus, who tells us in the Gospel that he has "authority on earth to forgive sins," has entrusted this authority to his Church. We speak of "going to confession." For many people it is something like going to the dentist: something we don't particularly like to do, which may hurt us. We know it is good for us, however, and afterwards we feel better.

131

The Sacrament of Penance is so much more than that. It is a personal encounter with One who loves us beyond our imagining; a meeting no less momentous than that between the paralytic and Jesus in the crowded house, where the babble of conversation was suddenly hushed as everyone present held his breath to see what Jesus would say and do.

We confess our sins to the priest. And the priest pronounces absolution. In reality, however, it is *Jesus* to whom we recite the sorry tale of how we have let him down, and let others down. *He* is the one who lifts the burden of guilt from our shoulders. The priest is only his representative.

So often we take this forgiveness for granted. If we realized the wonder of it, we would say with the people in today's Gospel: "We have never seen anything like this!" What have we done to deserve this forgiveness? Is it God's reward for the humiliation of confessing our sins to a fellow sinner? Certainly not. Nothing *we* do can ever "make up" for our sins. Jesus alone was able to pay the price of sin. He did so on Calvary. God's forgiveness is free. But it is not cheap. It cost Jesus Christ his life's blood.

Jesus offers us this costly but free gift of forgiveness out of *love*: not our love for him (which is weak, intermittent, and imperfect); no, the source and motive of our forgiveness is the Lord's love for us — which is total, eternal, and all-consuming. The body and blood of Christ, given to us here in the Eucharist, are not a reward for services rendered. Even after a good confession we still have to say: "Lord, I am not worthy. . ." The Eucharist is medicine for sick sinners; food that strengthens us to journey on another day, another week, another month; until finally our journey ends with the summons home. Then sacraments will cease and be no more. Then we shall see our crucified and risen Lord face to face.

Eighth Sunday of the Year

Hosea 2:16-17, 21-22; Mark 2:18-22

"I WILL ESPOUSE YOU TO ME FOREVER."

• *To show that Jesus Christ searches for us before we seek him; and that he offers us not just a better life, but a new life.*

We live today in what is called "a secular age," and "a secular society." The world in which we live does not necessarily deny God. It simply regards God and spiritual values (like love, self-sacrifice, humility) as optional extras, for people who happen to like that kind of thing. Our society attaches central importance only to things which can be touched, seen, measured, bought and sold.

All the great world religions agree in teaching that these material things alone can never bring us happiness. Hence the world's religions are concerned with the search for what lies beyond materialism, with the search for God. To this general statement there is one important exception, however. Christianity, and its parent Judaism, are concerned not with our search for God, but with *God's search for us*.

This is the theme of today's first reading. The prophet Hosea was addressing people who, like so many people today, were seeking happiness in material things. Hosea reproved the people for attributing their prosperity to their own efforts and good fortune. They had forgotten that everything they had was God's gift. God had rescued them from slavery in Egypt. He had guided them in their desert wanderings and given them "a land flowing with milk and honey," to use the biblical phrase. Instead of being grateful for these blessings, however, the people of Hosea's day had made wealth, power and pleasure their highest goals. This was idolatry: worshiping false gods rather than the one true God, from whom all good things come — wealth, power and pleasure included.

Hosea warned that God was angry at his people for their ingratitude. Yet God also wanted to cure the people of their evil ways. Because he was not only a righteous but also a loving God, Hosea explained, he would pursue his unfaithful people and win them back. God would restore what Hosea called the "pure love" his people had shown for God during their desert wanderings, following their deliverance from Egypt. The harsh conditions of that nomadic period of their national history excluded temptations from the false gods of materialism. Hosea represents God addressing the people as a loving and patient husband might speak to his unfaithful bride.

> I will lead her back into the desert and speak to her heart. She shall respond there as in the days of her youth, when she came up from the land of Egypt. I will espouse you in right and in justice, in love and in mercy. I will espouse you in fidelity, and you shall know the Lord.

According to that promise the people would "know" God not merely with their heads but with their hearts: as lovers know each other, and husbands and wives. They would know God as a God of love, because they would *experience* his love in a deep and personal way.

What God promised through Hosea he fulfilled through Jesus Christ. In today's Gospel solemn religious people came to Jesus to ask why his followers paid so little attention to the rules of fasting then in force. Jesus responded by telling his long-faced critics that as long as he was present fasting was as out of the question for his followers as it would be for guests at a wedding banquet. Now, Jesus said, was a time not for fasting, but for celebrating. Jesus wanted people to understand that, in and through him, God was doing something entirely *new*. The fasting rules cited by his critics belonged to the past. Jesus had ushered in the future.

To drive home this point, Jesus used two of those vivid images from everyday life that were so characteristic of his teaching. Who would use expensive new cloth, Jesus asked, to patch a tattered old coat? Who would pour new wine, which was still fermenting, into dried-up old wineskins? The skins would burst and the wine would be lost. No, new wine must be put into new wineskins.

"Can't you see?" Jesus was asking his critics. "Can't you understand?" In and through him God was doing something new. The Scriptures said that God would never forsake his people; that despite all their unfaithfulness and ingratitude he would never let them go. God would go after them and bring them back to himself. In him, Jesus declared, those prophecies were being fulfilled. In him God was offering not merely a *better* life, but a completely *new* life.

Jesus offers us no less today: not just improvement, not mere encouragement, not moral and spiritual uplift; but *radical change* — something *completely new*. What we could never do for ourselves, Jesus will do *for* us — *if* we will let him. Jesus is the representative and Son of God whose love will never let us go. In him we encounter this love. God is not someone who confronts us with stern moral lectures, with threats of punishment if we do not obey. God confronts us with an appeal: the appeal of *love*.

Because love can be rejected, the person who loves is always vulnerable. God loves us enough to make himself vulnerable. Think of the infant at Bethlehem, weak and vulnerable as all babies are. God loves us enough to expose himself to ridicule, rejection, crucifixion. The cross, like the manger, is a picture of God's love. "There is no greater love than this," Jesus says, "that a man should lay down his life for his friends" (John 15:13).

The cross is God's last and final appeal for an answering love on our side which will be at least a pale reflection of the love of God for us displayed by Jesus on the cross. The Good Friday liturgy frames this appeal in words taken from the Jewish Scriptures: "Is it nothing to you, all you who pass by? Look and see if there be any sorrow like my sorrow" (Lamentations 1:12).

The new life that Jesus offers us is his *own* life. He offers us this new life here in the Eucharist: in his holy word, in his broken body and poured out blood, given to us under the outward forms of bread and wine. As we receive these gifts we encounter him whom the writer of the final book of the Bible glimpsed in a vision seated upon a heavenly throne and saying: "Behold, I make all things new" (Revelation 21:5).

Jesus Christ is the only one who can make all things new. Jesus Christ does make all things new. Jesus Christ wants to make *your* life new — and mine. There is one thing, and one thing alone, which can prevent his doing so: our own deliberate and final refusal.

Ninth Sunday of the Year

Deuteronomy 5:12-15; Mark 2:23-3:6

"THE SON OF MAN IS LORD EVEN OF THE SABBATH."

• *To contrast religious legalism with the freedom of the Gospel, and to invite the hearers to deeper conversion.*

No aspect of Jesus' ministry so enraged the religious leaders of his day as his frequent disregard of the strict rules about Sabbath observance. Today's Gospel gives two examples. Jesus first defends his disciples for pulling off heads of grain as they walk through a field on the Sabbath. This was considered "harvest labor," one of the thirty-nine kinds of work forbidden on the Sabbath in Jesus' day. Jesus then magnifies his offense, in the eyes of his critics, by healing a man with a withered hand on the Sabbath.

The Jewish Scriptures give two reasons for resting from work on the Sabbath. We heard one in today's first reading. This said that the Sabbath rest commemorated God's gift to his people of a permanent rest from their grinding servitude in Egypt. According to another explanation the Sabbath commemorated God's rest on the seventh day, after the six days of creation (see Exodus 20:11; 31:17).

There is no need to choose between these two explanations. Both express the fundamental reason for observing the Sabbath: It reminded the Jews of their special relationship with God. The Sabbath was the weekly memorial of the goodness, kindness, and mercy that God had shown both in creation and in delivering his people from bondage in Egypt.

Jesus' freedom with regard to Sabbath observance makes

two statements. The first concerns the purpose and importance of all religious laws. The second is a statement about who Jesus is.

Since the Sabbath was the weekly reminder of God's goodness, kindness and mercy, any interpretation of the Sabbath law that kept people from showing these qualities to others must be wrong. That is the point of Jesus' question:

> Is it permitted to do a good deed on the Sabbath — or an evil one? To preserve life — or to destroy it?

The silence of Jesus' critics shows that despite their legalism they still recognized that the Sabbath was meant to promote goodness, kindness, and mercy by reminding people of these qualities in God.

Jesus' healing of the man with the withered hand on the Sabbath violated the letter of the law, but fulfilled its spirit. Legalists could claim, however, that since the man's illness was not life-threatening, Jesus should have waited till the Sabbath was over to heal him. Indeed, in a similar incident in Luke's Gospel, the president of the synagogue told his congregation precisely that: "There are six working days: Come and be cured on one of them, not on the Sabbath" (Luke 13:14).

Jesus rejected that argument. To meet a human need or to relieve suffering, Jesus never hesitated to violate the letter of the law. It was his way of showing that people are more important than laws.

It is easy for us to feel superior to all this legalistic haggling over religious rules. Actually, the mentality against which Jesus protested is not as remote from us as we may suppose. Within the memory of many people here, Catholics — includ-

138

ing little children — were advised not to brush their teeth before attending a Mass at which they intended to receive Communion. If they accidentally swallowed a few drops of water, thus breaking the strict fast from midnight, they would not be allowed to receive Communion that day.

Those of us old enough to remember that and the many other legalistic rules that used to govern Catholic life as recently as 1960 smile when we recall those things now. Their consequences are still with us, however. There are still many Catholics for whom the practice of their religion is a source not of joy, but of fear and anxiety. They worry about not finding their way through a maze of rules. They fear that God will punish them if they make a mistake, even out of forgetfulness. They confess things that are no sins at all, and agonize over sins that have been forgiven long ago — as if God's forgiveness were not total, as if he made us work off our sins a little bit at a time. All that is the direct opposite of the good news of the Gospel.

Anxiety and fear in the practice of religion have their origin in legalism. Rules originally intended to help people get close to God can become, especially for sensitive people, obstacles *between* them and God. The legalistic observance of the Sabbath in Jesus' day was such an obstacle. By interpreting the law with a freedom that shocked the legalists, Jesus wanted to bring them back to the law's true purpose. As he said himself: "The sabbath was made for man, not man for the sabbath."

On a deeper level still, Jesus' violation of the Sabbath law was a statement about *who he was*. Jesus himself was a far more effective reminder of God's goodness, kindness and mercy than even the best observance of the Sabbath. This is the meaning of Jesus' second statement in today's Gospel: "The Son of man is lord even of the Sabbath."

It is no accident that Mark placed this story about Jesus and the Sabbath immediately after the question put to him by critics in last Sunday's Gospel: "Why do John's disciples and those of the Pharisees fast while yours do not?" (Mark 2:18).

In Jesus' day people fasted to support their prayer for the coming of God's anointed servant, the promised Messiah. Now that he had come, Jesus said, there was no need to fast. It was a time to celebrate. The old fasting rules belonged to the past. Jesus had inaugurated the future.

Similarly with the Sabbath. By pointing to God it pointed also, even if obscurely, to the one God had promised to send: his Messiah. Now the Messiah was here! His coming fulfilled the old Sabbath promise. He was lord of the Sabbath. In his presence the old arguments about what was permitted and forbidden on the Sabbath were irrelevant — just as the old fasting rules were now irrelevant. Fasting and haggling over rules should be replaced, Jesus told his critics, by rejoicing and doing good to others. This meant sharing with them *God's* goodness. To the goodness God had shown in creation and in the deliverance of his people from Egypt God had now added the greatest of all his acts of goodness: the gift of his Son, the promised Messiah.

There is one feature of the story we have not yet considered. Before healing the man with the withered hand, Mark tells us, Jesus "was deeply grieved that they had closed their minds against him." Which of us has not at some time grieved the Lord by closing *our* minds against him? By refusing his newness, his healing power, the liberating power of his love?

140

Jesus who is lord of the Sabbath wants to be our own personal Lord and Master as well. He will never force himself on us, however. With a patience that is as great as his all-consuming love for us, Jesus waits for us to acknowledge him as Lord — to say our personal Yes to him. When we do, he changes our lives — forever.

Tenth Sunday of the Year

Genesis 3:9-15; Mark 3:20-35

CHRIST'S TRUE FAMILY.

* *To explain the difficulties in today's Gospel, and to show that Christ's true relatives are those who try do his will.*

Sometimes the Bible seems very difficult to understand. Take today's Gospel, for instance. It contains three apparently unrelated units. In the first Jesus refutes the charge of his critics that he casts out demons by the power of the prince of demons. In the second he speaks about an unforgivable sin against the Holy Spirit. In the third Jesus explains that the true members of his family are not those related to him by blood, but those who try to do his will.

Where is the common theme between these three different units? And even if we take them separately, each has its own difficulties. Jesus' saying about demons has little meaning for us who live in a scientific age that explains sickness and evil as the result of natural causes, not of demonic influence. The saying about an unforgivable sin against the Holy Spirit seems to contradict what we have been taught about the possibility of forgiveness for *every* sin. And finally, Jesus' words about his true relatives seem almost insulting toward his mother and other family members. Is there any way we can make sense of all this?

Let's start with the apparent lack of unity between these three units. This is explained by the nature of the Gospels themselves. They are not like modern biographies. Rather they are collections of the stories about Jesus' life and teaching that circulated in the early Christian communities in the years following his death and resurrection.

Each of the four gospel writers selected from this material those elements that best suited his purpose. This explains, for instance, why only Matthew and Luke say anything about Jesus' birth and infancy; also why John gives no account of the institution of the Eucharist at the Last Supper, but only of the foot-washing — which the other three Gospels do not mention at all.

The gospel writers were responsible not only for the selection of their material, but also for its *arrangement*. The so-called Sermon on the Mount in chapters 5-7 of Matthew's Gospel, for instance, was composed by Matthew from authentic but most likely originally separate sayings of Jesus that had been preserved in the Christian community for which Matthew wrote. Today's Gospel is similar. Mark has combined three examples of Jesus' teaching that may originally have been given on quite different occasions. This explains the seeming lack of unity between them.

The first of the three examples contains Jesus' response to the charge that he casts out demons by the power of the prince of demons. In the New Testament demons represent all the powers and influences in the world that try to obstruct or destroy God's rule. Jesus had come, however, to *restore* God's rule — against which humankind had rebelled through self-will, as we heard in the first reading. If Jesus were really, as his critics charged, in league with those enemies of God's will that the New Testament calls "demons," he would be acting against the very purpose of his coming. This was clearly an absurdity and hence impossible.

What about the second unit in today's Gospel, Jesus' teaching about an unforgivable sin against the Holy Spirit? Throughout the Bible God's Spirit is presented as the divine power at work in the world to heal the damage caused by sin. To sin against the Spirit means to deny that God is at work in the world at all. This was what Jesus' critics were doing when they charged that he performed his miracles of healing through a pact with the devil.

Sin against the Spirit is not some isolated deed — certainly not one that a person can commit without knowing it. It means a fixed state of mind, culpable blindness, deliberate refusal to acknowledge and accept God's saving work. The person who adopts this state of mind places himself, by a free choice, *outside* God's saving work by rejecting it and refusing to have anything to do with it.

In saying that this sin is "unforgivable," Jesus simply means that people who deliberately choose to exclude themselves from the sphere of God's saving work will find that God respects their choice. God will not force himself upon them. Jesus does not say whether such a rejection of God is necessarily permanent. Elsewhere, however, he says that what is impossible for man is possible for God (Mark 10:27).

This brings us to the final part of today's Gospel: Jesus' teaching about his true family. This was occasioned by the message that Jesus' mother and other relatives were outside asking for him. He responds with a rhetorical question: "Who are my mother and my brothers?" According to *our* way of thinking, this implies that they were unimportant, of no account. In reality, Jesus was using a well-known Jewish form of exaggeration for the sake of emphasis.

What seems to us like a rejection of his relatives was actually Jesus' way of asserting in a forceful way that there was

144

a deeper basis for relationship to him than that based on blood. This is the obedient acceptance of God's rule by people who try to do his will.

The Man and Woman in the first reading rebelled against God's rule. So did those forces hostile to God called "demons" in the first part of the Gospel. So, finally, do those who "sin against the Holy Spirit" by denying that God acts in the world at all.

Mark tells us that Jesus' words about his true relatives were spoken as Jesus "gazed around him at those seated in the circle." Are *we* in that circle? Are we listening to Jesus' words? Are we honestly trying to do his will?

If we are, then Jesus' words are spoken to *us*. We are truly brother, sister and mother to Jesus Christ. That, dear sisters and brothers in the Lord, is his good news. That is the Gospel of the Lord.

Eleventh Sunday of the Year

Ezekiel 17:22-24; 2 Corinthians 5:6-10; Mark 4:26-34

"THE SEED GROWS WITHOUT HIS KNOWING HOW."

• *To counter discouragement by helping the hearers to focus on God's power.*

"This is how it is with the reign of God." What does Jesus mean? What *is* this "reign of God" — or "kingdom of God," as it is often translated — that we hear so much about in the Gospels?

God's reign or kingdom denotes a world in which those sayings of Jesus called the Beatitudes are fulfilled: where the sorrowful are consoled, the meek inherit the earth, those who hunger and thirst for justice are satisfied, the merciful experience the mercy they have shown to others, the pure hearted see God, the peacemakers are known as God's daughters and sons, and those who previously were persecuted for the cause of right are finally vindicated. (See Matthew 5:3-10.)

From the dawn of history, people have dreamed of such a world. The Bible calls it God's kingdom and describes it in parables. We heard one in today's first reading. When God's kingdom comes, Ezekiel said, God would take the weakest and most delicate shoot from one of the mighty cedar trees of Lebanon and make of it a tree more noble than all the rest.

It shall put forth branches and bear fruit . . .
Birds of every kind shall dwell beneath it.

Because such a thing was, by all normal standards, impossible, when it happened everyone would recognize it as God's work, Ezekiel declared.

146

Thus says the Lord God: ... All the trees of the field shall know that I, the Lord, bring low the high tree, lift high the lowly tree, and make the withered tree bloom.

Ezekiel's parable was a message of hope to his dispirited countrymen in exile in Babylon. Like one of the lofty Lebanon cedars felled by the woodsman's axe, their once mighty nation had been cut down. Humanly speaking, there was no hope that it could ever be restored. Yet God would bring his people back again to their own land, in his own time and in his own way. He would take the most delicate shoot from the fallen tree to make of it a great nation.

Jesus' parable in today's Gospel about the tiny mustard seed that "springs up to become the largest of shrubs, with branches big enough for the birds of the sky to build nests in its shade" builds on the foundation laid by Ezekiel. Like him, Jesus was speaking to people who were dispirited and without hope.

Jesus began his public ministry in this Gospel according to Mark by announcing that God's long awaited kingdom had arrived. (See 1:15.) What actually came, however, was a far cry from the divine kingdom foretold by Ezekiel and the other prophets. Jesus' followers were unimpressive: a small band of ignorant fishermen with little education and less influence. The upright pillars of the establishment held both Jesus and his followers in open contempt. "He eats with tax collectors and sinners," they said scornfully (Mark 2:16). How could anyone take seriously the claim of this self-appointed rabbi from Nazareth that he, of all people, had come to announce the arrival of God's kingdom of justice and peace?

The parable of the great bush growing from a tiny mustard seed was Jesus' response to his critics. It also contained a message of hope for those followers of Jesus who had begun to suspect that his critics were right. The kingdom he had come to proclaim, Jesus said, could no more be judged by his admittedly humble beginnings than one could draw from inspection of a tiny mustard seed a picture of the great shrub it would produce.

The other parable, of the seed growing secretly, is similar. Once the farmer casts the seed in the ground, he can do nothing to promote or hasten its growth. The process of germination and development takes place without his help, without his knowledge even.

> He goes to bed and gets up day after day. Through it all the seed sprouts and grows *without his knowing how it happens.*

Jesus addressed this parable to those among his followers who were disillusioned because he was not the glamorous and powerful national hero they wanted the Messiah to be. Why didn't he *act*, they asked? Why didn't he lead a revolution to overthrow the hated Roman military government of occupation?

To all such doubters Jesus said, in effect: "Look at the farmer. He waits patiently for the time of harvest. God's harvest is coming also, God's hour. He has made the decisive beginning. I have sown the seed. Because it is *God's* seed, the harvest is certain."

Was it only in Jesus' lifetime that his followers had doubts? How much of the Church's work today seems to be an exercise in futility! No wonder we often grow discouraged. No wonder that many people become disillusioned and cynical. Doesn't the state of the Church today give us every reason for discouragement and cynicism?

148

Those of us old enough to remember Pope John XXIII know it does not. It is reported that "good Pope John," as he was called, liked to conclude his night prayers by saying: "It's your Church, Lord. I'm going to bed." How wise that is. If the Church is God's and not ours (and it is), then the success or failure of the Church's work is not determined by us. Today, no less than in Jesus' earthly lifetime, it is he, the Lord, who sows the seed. It is he who will bring the seed to fruition. Our task is to be patient, as Jesus was patient; to remain serenely confident, as he remained confident even to his final hour on Calvary. There it was Jesus and not his enemies who spoke the last word — a word not of defeat but of victory: "It is finished" (John 19:30).

Here in the Eucharist we have with us the One who spoke that word. Here his finished work is celebrated and made available to us: the work of proclaiming and bringing in God's kingdom. Here we who in baptism became members of that kingdom enjoy its fruits: forgiveness of our sins, reconciliation with the One those sins have offended and with each other; love, joy, and the Lord's peace. Here we can repeat Paul's words in our second reading:

> We continue to be confident. . . . We walk by faith, not by sight. . . . We are full of confidence. . .

Twelfth Sunday of the Year

Job 38:1, 8-11; Mark 4:35-41

"WHY ARE YOU LACKING IN FAITH?"

• *To deepen the hearers' faith.*

A few years ago a British actor scored a great theatrical success with a one-man show entitled, "The Gospel according to Mark." Standing on a bare stage, without costumes and props, and using only the simplest gestures and his voice for dramatic effect, he recited by memory the whole of Mark's Gospel. Audiences on both sides of the Atlantic remained fascinated for over two hours.

An important ingredient in this success was the actor's skill. At least as important, however, was the text itself. Mark's Gospel, the shortest and seemingly the simplest of the four, is a work of great artistry. From the many different stories, sayings, and incidents in the life of Jesus current in his own Christian community, Mark compiled a unified narrative of rare dramatic power. Reading the Gospel in bits and pieces, as we do in church, we easily overlook Mark's achievement. Today's Gospel is a good example.

The version we just heard began: "One day as evening drew on, Jesus said . . ." Mark's original text ties the story closely to what has preceded: "and he said to them on *that* day, in the evening . . ." The day, in Mark's description, began with Jesus teaching people by the lakeshore. To avoid being overwhelmed by the crowd, Jesus got into a boat to put a little distance between himself and his hearers. He then told several parables, of which the most important was the familiar story of the sower and the seed.

150

Mark concludes this section by indicating that what he has recorded was typical of Jesus' teaching. "With many such parables he would give them his message, so far as they were able to receive it. He never spoke to them except in parables; but privately to his disciples he explained everything" (4:33-34).

What follows was intended by Mark as a continuation of Jesus' private explanation to his disciples: in deeds this time, rather than in words.

These explanatory deeds begin with Jesus sound asleep in the middle of the storm — the only place in the Gospels, incidentally, where we see Jesus sleeping. It was the sleep of exhaustion after a busy day. But it was also the tranquil rest of the only one in that boat who had no reason for fear amid the elemental forces of nature.

Though the disciples were experienced seamen, Mark says nothing about any measure to ensure the safety of the vessel and her crew. Instead these seasoned fishermen turn in panic to their sleeping Master, who unlike them was no sailor, with the reproachful question: "Teacher, doesn't it matter to you that we are going to drown?"

Without a word of reply, Jesus acts. In language identical to that already used to describe a healing at Capernaum (1:25), Mark writes: "He rebuked the wind and said to the sea; 'Quiet! Be still!' " Jesus had already shown that he is Lord over sickness. Now he shows that he rules wind and wave as well.

Repeatedly the Jewish Scriptures ascribed this power to God alone. Today's readings contain two examples. In the first, God speaks of his work in creation:

Who shut within doors the sea . . . and said: Thus far shall you

151

come but no farther, and here shall your proud waves be
stilled?

The responsorial psalm was similar. Recounting a scene of
mariners in distress, the psalmist offers what could be a commentary on the Gospel: "They cried to the Lord in their distress; from their straits he rescued them. He hushed the
storm to a gentle breeze, and the billows of the sea were
stilled" (Psalm 107:28-29).

The "calm" that Mark mentions following Jesus' rebuke to
wind and wave was not only the stillness of nature. There was
an eerie silence in the boat as well, as Jesus' disciples looked
at each other in amazement, each formulating the same question: "Who can this be that the wind and the sea obey him?"
Remember — their Scriptures told them that only *God* could
do what they had just seen Jesus do.

The first to break the silence, however, was Jesus. In this
story, which consists almost entirely of questions, it was now
his turn. "Why are you so terrified?" Jesus asked. "Why are
you lacking in faith?" Mark wanted his readers to hear Jesus
addressing these challenging questions not only to his friends
in the boat, but to *them* — to his friends in all ages, ourselves
included.

From the earliest times Christians have compared the
Church to a ship. Like the ark which rescued Noah and his
family from the great flood, the Church preserves us from the
flood of danger and evil in the world. Time and again, however, our ship is buffeted by storms. The Lord seems to be
absent — or at least indifferent. Like those first friends of
Jesus in the storm on the lake, we cry out not in faith, but in
fear. At the proper time — which is his time, not ours — the

Lord banishes the danger, and with it our cause for fear. Having done so, he challenges us with his insistent question: "Why are you lacking in faith?"

The answering question of Jesus' friends in the Gospel, "Who can this be that the wind and the sea obey him?" is a pre-Easter question. The friends of Jesus in the boat had not yet seen the risen Lord. We, who here encounter the risen Lord in his holy word, and in the sacrament of his body and blood, know him *better* than those first friends of his. This man, Jesus of Nazareth, the son of Mary, is our elder brother and our best friend. Yet he is also God's Son. If Jesus could demand faith of those friends in the boat, who knew him only as one like themselves, how much more can he demand this same faith of us, who also know him as one *unlike* ourselves.

"Why are you lacking in faith?" Jesus asks us. What better response could we make than to pray, like another friend of Jesus in this Gospel according to Mark:

"Lord, I believe. Help my unbelief" (9:24).

Thirteenth Sunday of the Year

Mark 5:21-43

"DO NOT FEAR, ONLY BELIEVE."

• *By explaining the difference between superstition and faith, to deepen faith.*

People who suffer from an incurable illness can become so desperate that they are willing to try anything. In recent years we have witnessed the campaign for the legalization of laetrile as a supposed cure for cancer, despite medical evidence that it is worthless. From time to time the media report about desperately ill people journeying to clinics in countries like Mexico or Russia in search of medical treatment not available to them at home.

The woman in today's Gospel who had suffered for twelve years from a hemorrhage was similarly desperate.

> She had received treatment at the hands of doctors of every sort and exhausted her savings in the process, yet she got no relief; on the contrary, she only grew worse.

She approached Jesus as a last resort. After so many bitter disappointments, she hardly dared to hope for a cure — but what did she have to lose?

Her situation was even more desperate than we can realize. According to the religious law of the day, the woman's illness excluded her from fellowship with God's people. She was ritually unclean, and anyone who touched her became similarly defiled (see Leviticus 15:25-27). She was deliberately violating this quarantine when she mixed with the crowd and tried to touch Jesus. This was a message of her desperation. Her real interest, however, was less in Jesus' *person* than in his reputed *power*. "If I just touch his clothes," the woman thought, "I shall get well." What looks at first sight like faith turns out on closer examination to be little better than superstition.

The woman's fear as soon as Jesus realized that she had violated the law by touching him shows how far she was from true faith.

> Fearful and beginning to tremble now . . . the woman came and fell in front of him and told him the whole truth.

Faith is trust in a person. It is the opposite of fear. Superstition, on the other hand, is reliance on a power which, if not handled correctly, can become harmful. Hence superstition contains a large element of fear.

Notice how Jesus treated the woman. Instead of scolding her, he encouraged her. Realizing her desperation, Jesus judged the woman's action more generously than it actually deserved. To this poor soul huddled at his feet in fear Jesus spoke words of reassurance.

> Daughter, it is your faith that has cured you. Go in peace and be free of this illness.

By treating the woman *as if* she had faith, when in reality she had little more than superstition, Jesus planted in her the seed of true faith. Jesus spoke as if the healing were the *consequence* of the woman's faith. In reality her healing was the *cause* and beginning of true faith for this desperate woman.

Following her healing Mark at once resumes the narrative of the gravely ill girl, which he has interrupted to relate the healing of the woman with the hemorrhage. Jesus' words to the grief-stricken father, who had just learned of his daughter's death, link what follows to the experience of the fearful woman for whom Jesus had just opened the door to faith. "Do not fear," Jesus tells Jairus. "Only believe" [thus the original Greek].

We need not linger over the details of this second and greater miracle. Mark's purpose in relating it was not so much to preserve the historical record as to make a theological statement about who Jesus is. This statement begins with Jesus' words to the mourners at Jairus' house: "The child is not dead. She is asleep." This is less a medical statement than a religious one. For him who has power to raise the dead, Jesus was saying, physical death is no more significant than sleep. What follows illustrates this statement.

These two intertwined stories have a common theme. Both speak of fear and of faith. Fear shrinks from encountering the one we fear — as the woman shrank from Jesus once he sensed that she had violated the law of quarantine. Faith *seeks* encounter with its object. As long as the woman was motivated by superstition, her encounter with Jesus had to be secret, because of the fear arising from her superstitious trust in Jesus' healing power. Jesus invited her, however, to move beyond superstition to faith. Faith, like love, casts out fear (see 1 John 4:18).

"Do not fear. Only believe." Jesus' words to the bereaved father, Jairus, were spoken in the face of the thing we all fear most of all: death. Jesus speaks the same words to us today. He invites us to move from fear to faith. How fearful many Catholics are! Some fear God as a stern judge waiting to punish them for the slightest infraction of the rules. Others fear

156

not God but themselves; their inadequacy, their weakness, their inability to keep the rules.

What do *you* fear? We all fear something. Jesus is inviting you to move beyond fear, to faith. When you do, you open the door to him who is able to do, in you and through you, not merely the unexpected, not merely the improbable — but the *impossible*!

Fourteenth Sunday of the Year

Ezekiel 2:2-5; 2 Corinthians 12:7-10; Mark 6:1-6

"THEY FOUND HIM TOO MUCH FOR THEM."

• *To challenge the hearers to respond to Jesus Christ as we encounter him in his church.*

On this Independence Day weekend we celebrate more than two centuries of national history. We Americans have a reputation among the peoples of the world for optimism. Our country's history has taught us to be optimistic. Until the Vietnam War it seemed that just about every major problem confronting us was soluble. From small beginnings we became the richest and most powerful nation on earth. As we look out today, however, on a world filled more with shadows than with light, we wonder how long this success story can continue.

Today's readings are not about success and power, however. They deal with rejection and weakness. In the first reading we heard God's warning to the prophet Ezekiel that his own people would reject the prophet's message. The second reading recorded Paul's prayer for deliverance from what he called "a thorn in the flesh": some handicap, a physical ailment, or a feeling of inadequacy. God answered this prayer not by taking away Paul's burden, but by giving him the strength to bear it. Through this experience of personal weakness, Paul writes, he learned to appreciate God's power.

Finally, in the Gospel, we saw Jesus rejected by the people who knew him best. "They found him too much for them," our text said. This is a free rendering of Mark's original: "They were scandalized at him." Jesus scandalized people in three ways. For some he was too close to them, too ordinary. "Isn't this the *carpenter*?" people asked derisively. "Don't we know his family and relatives? What makes *him* so special?"

Others found Jesus too remote, too "different."

Where did he get all this? What kind of wisdom is he endowed with? How is it such miraculous deeds are accomplished by his hands?

People who reacted to Jesus like that were scandalized because he was not ordinary enough. Some of them, Mark tells us elsewhere, even thought Jesus was out of his mind (see 3:21).

Still others were scandalized because Jesus seemed so weak. This was the judgment of the bystanders at Calvary who jeered: "You would pull the temple down, would you, and build it in three days? Come down from the cross and save yourself!" (Mark 15:29)

Such taunts were the final judgment of Jesus' contemporaries on this man who seemed to make himself equal with God, yet who, when the chips were down, was unable to save himself from a criminal's death.

By all normal standards Jesus' life was anything but a success story. Most of his contemporaries found him quite unimpressive. That was true then. It remains true today. To be sure, Jesus no longer comes to people in his human body. Since his resurrection and ascension Jesus Christ comes to people through his *mystical* body, the Church. People encounter and judge Jesus today through those who have become members of his body in baptism — in other words, through us. *We* are eyes, ears, hands, feet and voice for Jesus Christ. He has no other.

Many people today say they accept Jesus Christ, but want nothing to do with his Church. For some the Church is too ordinary. They complain that the Church is full of hypocrites, people who are no better than anyone else.

Other people find the Church too remote. They say it is hopelessly out of date. They complain that the Church preaches irrelevant dogmas to people who need practical help to cope with life's problems. They are scandalized because the Church seems to lack compassion for people who cannot live up to unrealistically high moral standards.

Still others find the Church too weak to command their respect. Why doesn't the Church *do something*, they ask, about the terrible problems of our society: urban poverty and blight in the richest country on earth, the arms race, crime and terrorism, injustice, greed and the rape of the environment?

People today, in short, are scandalized by the Church for reasons very similar to those that caused Jesus' contemporaries to be scandalized at him. Many people today seek a "pure" Church: one that is not ordinary, not remote, not weak. Some believe they have found this purity in a congregation of "born again Christians" that deliberately excludes the lax and lukewarm. Others find the purity they are seeking in the electronic church. On television the worshipers are all squeaky clean. The preacher always has a polished and uplifting message. The singing is always fervent and on key. How many parish churches can compete with that?

The Catholic Church does not even try to compete. Like its Lord, the Catholic Church is, most of the time, very ordinary and unimpressive. It is the Church of saints. Yet it is also the Church of sinners. It stubbornly insists on making room for people like you and me who slip and fall and compromise; who are weak in faith; whose faith at times is hard to distinguish from superstition.

The Catholic Church, in short, is human, as Jesus was human. It is ordinary, as he was ordinary. It can seem remote, as Jesus sometimes seemed remote. It is often weak, as Jesus was weak. Hidden behind this ordinariness and remoteness and weakness, however, is all the power of God; all the compassion of his Son Jesus; and all the strength of his Holy Spirit, who came in fiery tongues on the first Pentecost to kindle a fire that is still burning; and to sweep people off their feet with a rushing mighty wind that is still blowing.

Most of Jesus' contemporaries were scandalized at him. "They found him too much for them." What about *you*?

Fifteenth Sunday of the Year

Amos 7:12-15; Mark 6:7-13

SOCIAL JUSTICE.

- *To show the nature and need of prophecy, and of repentance.*

Should the Church get involved in politics? Many people say it should not. "Religion and politics don't mix," they contend. Others disagree. Politics, they point out, is about life. A religion that is unwilling to leave the sacristy and go out into the marketplace has nothing to say about real life. Such a religion is irrelevant, these people argue. Whenever fundamental moral principles are at stake, they contend, the Church *must* speak out. Otherwise the Church risks being untrue to its Lord and his message.

But which political questions actually do involve moral issues so important as to justify or require Church involvement? Was the Vietnam War such an issue? For many it was. Religious leaders were in the vanguard of those who brought about the end of our country's involvement in Vietnam. Ironically, the same powerful organs of public opinion which welcomed Church intervention in the debate over the Vietnam War angrily denounce Church leaders who today try to end the abortionists' war against society's weakest and most defenseless group: the unborn. Add to this example the current debate over nuclear arms, and we see how complex things become as soon as we do take our faith out of the sacristy and into the marketplace.

Today's first reading introduced a religious figure who was severely condemned for his involvement in politics. Like

Jesus, the prophet Amos was a layman with no professional training for religious office. "I was no prophet, nor have I belonged to the company of prophets," Amos told the priest in charge of the sanctuary at Bethel. God had called Amos while he was still a gardener and a shepherd and had commanded him: "Go, prophesy to my people Israel."

God gave Amos no crystal ball to predict future events. That is not the prophet's primary task. Instead Amos, like all the prophets, was summoned to speak a "word of the Lord" to people of his day: to warn, to admonish, to rebuke, and to encourage.

As a simple shepherd, Amos was scandalized by his glimpses of city life during his visits to market. He saw wealthy, callous plutocrats, overfed and overhoused, spending their time thinking up new ways to amuse themselves. Meanwhile poor peasants like Amos, burdened with debt, could be sold into slavery for the price of a pair of shoes.

Amos saw this glaring social injustice compounded at the religious sanctuary. There he found prosperous worshipers rejoicing in their good fortune, which they interpreted as proof of God's favor. To this rotten and decaying society the official prophets and priests had nothing to say but "smooth words and seductive visions" (Isaiah 30:10) — rather like certain religious speakers at prayer breakfasts of political and business leaders today.

Without mincing words, Amos pronounced his society ripe for God's judgment (8:2f). The official priest Amaziah roundly condemned Amos for this uncomfortable message, and for daring to speak at all in a religious sanctuary without official permission. With the contempt of the religious official for the upstart outsider Amaziah told Amos:

> Off with you, visionary. Never again prophesy in Bethel; for it
> is the king's sanctuary and a royal temple.

Amos' message had been rejected. Jesus spoke about such rejection in the Gospel as he sent out the Twelve to preach in his name.

> If any place will not receive you or hear you, shake its dust
> from your feet in testimony against them as you leave.

Elsewhere Jesus almost seemed to make rejection of his message by some, at least, a criterion by which to judge whether the message was being proclaimed faithfully. "Woe to you when all speak well of you; just so did their fathers treat the false prophets" (Luke 6:26).

What could have been less popular than the message of repentance he gave them in today's Gospel? "Repentance" in the New Testament means more than mere regret for past actions which are perceived by hindsight to be wrong. Repentance means a fundamental change of direction, a one hundred and eighty degree turn. Repentance means *turning around* from self to God. It means putting God at the *center* of life rather than somewhere out on the fringe.

Where is our need for repentance today? It is everywhere. Our present pope has repeatedly told us Americans, and people in other western countries as well, that we need to repent of *consumerism*. This is the error of thinking we can buy happiness by multiplying possessions. We need to repent too of self-indulgent *hedonism*: the mindless philosophy that says, "If it feels good, do it." We need to repent to the *hard-hearted selfishness* that ignores the need of the poor and oppressed in our midst; or that thinks our obligation to them can be discharged by gifts to charity out of our surplus wealth, with no examination of the unjust structures that cause poverty and oppression.

We need to repent of an *over-spiritualized religion* which is concerned simply with saying prayers and getting into heaven; which ignores the challenge to build colonies of heaven here on earth that is implicit in the words of Jesus' model prayer: "Your will be done on earth as it is in heaven."

We need to repent, finally, of the belief that we can achieve security through weapons that threaten life, whether it is a handgun bedside the bed at home, or intercontinental missiles poised to wipe out millions of people in another country at the touch of a button. A society, a nation, and a world that have no better means of security than these are a society, a nation, and a world already threatened by destruction and dissolution.

These are the "unclean spirits" against which the Lord sends us today. One weapon, and one weapon alone, can cast them out: *repentance*. The repentance to which Jesus summons us is not somewhere else, tomorrow. It is here, and it is now. And it begins not with someone else. If it is to begin at all, this repentance must begin with ourselves.

Sixteenth Sunday of the Year

Mark 6:30-34

"COME TO AN OUT-OF-THE-WAY PLACE
AND REST A LITTLE."

• *To help the hearers find spiritual refreshment amid the busyness of life.*

"What goes up must come down." This familiar saying is an example of life's fundamental rhythm. We see this rhythm in breathing, in waking and sleeping, in the alternation of the seasons, of work, and of rest. We see it in today's Gospel.

The Twelve have returned to Jesus after a time of arduous labor to report "all that they have done and what they have taught." Jesus knew that after this strenuous activity they needed to withdraw — time, we would say today, to recharge their spiritual batteries. Those who preach the Gospel can give to others only what they themselves have received. The apostles had given. Now they needed to receive. So Jesus invited them to "come by yourselves to an out-of-the-way place and rest a little."

This need for periodic withdrawal and rest was the reason for God's third commandment: "Remember to keep holy the Sabbath." The way we fulfill that commandment, and even the day, have changed from Jesus' day. The Christian Sabbath is not Saturday, but Sunday, the day on which Jesus was raised from the dead. Every Sunday is a "little Easter." We "keep holy" this Christian Sabbath by obeying Jesus' command to "do this in my memory." As we give thanks to God over the bread and wine, which symbolize our work and striving, God changes them through the power of his Holy Spirit into the body and blood of his risen Son. When we receive these now-transformed gifts, we are filled with all the power, goodness, and love of God himself. We call the celebration in which we do this "the Eucharist," a term that comes from the Greek word for "thanksgiving."

Once again, we, the Lord's people, have gathered on the Lord's Day for this celebration of Christian thanksgiving. For a time we step aside from the demands, the worries, the hustle and bustle of everyday life. Like the Twelve in today's Gospel, we too have come to "an out-of-the-way place to rest a little." The place in which we gather is "holy": it has been set apart from ordinary, everyday use and dedicated to God. We need this time together, as God's people, with him. We need the nourishment he gives us here at his two tables: the table of the word, and the table of the Lord's body and blood.

Jesus' loving invitation to come to an out-of-the-way place and rest a little is not only for Sunday. We need such times of spiritual refreshment during the week as well. The busier we are, the more important these times are. How can we find them? Here are a few suggestions.

In every life, no matter how crowded, there are empty times — times when we must wait. We wait in the checkout line at the supermarket. We wait in traffic. We must walk to and from the car at our place of work, or at a shopping center. Such empty periods in the day can be turned into "times for God." As you wait, as you walk to or from the car, lift up your heart and mind to God. Hold up to him those whom you love. Ask him to bless them in the way he knows they need to be blessed. Hold yourself before your heavenly Father with all your weakness and need, all the loose ends in your life, your brokenness, compromises, failures. Long prayers are not necessary. Simple, short prayers are best.

"Jesus, help me."
"My Lord and my God."
"Lord Jesus, I love you."
"Good Physician, make me whole."
"Mary, Mother, bless your child."

Or simply the holy names, "Jesus, Mary, Joseph" — or the holy name of Jesus alone — uttered reverently and with love in your heart — all these are perfect prayers that go straight to the loving heart of our heavenly Father.

It is even possible to turn your car into an out-of-the-way place where you can rest in God's presence. Turn off the car radio and pray the rosary as you drive down the highway. Or use one of the short prayers already suggested. Even better, create "islands of quiet" — times for God — at home or at work. Turn off the television and turn to God. Reach for your Bible or rosary instead of for a cigarette or a magazine. Take part of your lunch hour or coffee break at work to follow Jesus' invitation to rest with him in an out-of-the-way place. You will find him there already, waiting for you.

The more often you make time for the Lord in your life, the more you will discover that the words of today's responsorial psalm are true — true for *you*.

The Lord is my shepherd. I lack nothing.
In green pastures he gives me repose;
beside restful waters he leads me;
he refreshes my soul.

(Psalm 23:1-2)

168

Seventeenth Sunday of the Year

John 6:1-15

"WHAT GOOD IS THAT FOR SO MANY?"

• *To show that our meager resources are transformed when we offer them to God; yet that God's power is not at our disposal.*

More than one person here today comes with some burden or suffering. Perhaps it is a family problem, financial worry, or a personal difficulty. When you look at your life it seems to be a tangle of loose ends, broken resolutions, and failure. You ask: "Will my life ever be different, and better?" Deep in your heart you fear that the answer is "No." Add to whatever personal difficulties we bring here today, the problems of our country and of the world — economic uncertainty and the dread specter of nuclear war — and we have, seemingly, every reason for gloom and despair.

Today's Gospel describes a problem every bit as insoluble as any we face: the impossibility of feeding a vast crowd far from any source of food. Philip declares that the problem in fact is insoluble:

Not even with two hundred days' wages could we buy enough to give them a mouthful!

Philip is the perfect example of the person who, when faced with a difficulty, says immediately: "It's hopeless." Even when a solution is proposed, such a person will dismiss it at once. "Oh, *that's* no good. We've tried that before and it didn't work."

Another of Jesus' friends, Andrew, is a bit more practical.

Instead of concentrating on the magnitude of the problem, he first looks at the means for solving it. "There is *some* food. I saw a boy with five barley loaves and a couple of dried fish." Yet even Andrew realizes at once how pitifully inadequate these resources are to solve the problem, for he adds immediately: "But what good is that for so many?"

This little exchange between Jesus and his friends is merely the prelude to the story. Jesus wastes no time in discussion. Instead he acts. We must leave to the scripture scholars the question of "exactly what happened." The preacher's task is not so much to explain the gospel stories, as to interpret their spiritual significance. One interpretation is certain. When we place our resources, however inadequate they may be, in the hands of Jesus Christ, we discover that they are inadequate no longer.

You come here today with burdens and problems. Many of them may seem to you unbearable and insoluble. If you look only at your own strength, you realize that it is not enough to bear the burden. Your own resources are insufficient to solve your problems.

Offer those resources, however inadequate they may be, to Jesus Christ, and you will find that they are not inadequate. When to our weakness is added the strength and power of God, made available to us in his Son Jesus, then great things can happen in and through even people as weak and poor as ourselves.

Look *down* — at your problems, your woefully insufficient means of dealing with them, at your weakness of will, your inconstancy, your many compromises and constant falls — look down at all that, and you will have indeed every reason for discouragement, perhaps even for despair. Look *up*, however — up into the face of Jesus Christ, your divine Savior, but also your brother and your best friend; place your pitifully inadequate strength, which you know to be nothing but weakness, into his hands; and then you will find that the impossible happens. The burden which seems unbearable can be carried. The problem you thought insoluble may not disappear, but it will not ultimately defeat you. When we place our littleness unreservedly in the hands of Jesus Christ it becomes greatness. The impossible happens. Where before there had been only discouragement and despair, there is hope and joy.

It is tempting to stop there. But there is more spiritual significance in this story than the message of hope for those who think their situation is hopeless, and their problems insoluble. The people who experienced Jesus' miracle were so impressed that they wanted to capture his power, to make sure it would be available to them always. That is why they wanted to make Jesus a king. Here, they thought, was the one who could get the hated Roman government of occupation off their backs. The man who could feed such a vast crowd in the wilderness was surely capable of greater things still. In *this* expectation, however, the people were disappointed. Jesus "fled back to the mountain alone."

Jesus Christ is never at our disposal. We are at *his* disposal. The power of God, which is at work in Jesus, is not some kind of automatic solution that we can invoke when all else fails. We cannot "capture" Jesus Christ any more than the people in today's Gospel could capture him.

In Jesus there *is* power, certainly. It is not power, however, to do our own thing. Jesus empowers us to do *God's* thing. Jesus' power is the power of love. Love is creative. Once truly touched by love we become capable of things that previously seemed beyond us. Those who love, and are touched by love, sacrifice for those they love. They find they can run where before they could scarcely walk. *This* is the power of Jesus Christ: the creative power of love, a force which will not always transform our problems, but which will infallibly transform *us*, if we will but entrust ourselves to Jesus, and to his love, without reserve.

Here in the Eucharist, Jesus repeats the miracle recounted in today's Gospel. We, the hungry and weary people of God, are fed by Jesus Christ with bread in the wilderness of our earthly pilgrimage: that "daily bread" for which Jesus taught us to pray — nourishment, support, strength as we stumble onwards towards our heavenly homeland, lying down to rest each night a day's march nearer home.

Eighteenth Sunday of the Year

Exodus 16:2-4, 12-15; John 6:24-35

"THIS IS THE WORK OF GOD:

HAVE FAITH IN THE ONE HE SENT."

• *To deepen the hearers' faith.*

"This is the work of God," Jesus says in today's Gospel. "Have faith in the One he sent." What is your idea of faith? For many Catholics faith means a set of truths, such as we find in the creed that we recite every Sunday at Mass. These truths are properly called *the* faith. Faith itself is more than a list of truths to which we give mental assent. Faith is, first, *a personal relationship of trust.* It is an affair not just of the head, but also of the heart. Even the creed which contains the truths of faith begins not, "We believe *that*," but "We believe *in*." To believe in someone is to trust that person. Let me tell you a story about this kind of faith.

Some mountain guides in a Swiss village organized a climb late one autumn, after all the tourists had departed. They reached their chosen summit without difficulty. They were disappointed, however, not to have found an edelweiss, the star-shaped delicate white flower that grows only at high altitudes and is prized by mountaineers as a souvenir.

The group had already started their descent when one of them spotted a single edelweiss on a ledge some thirty feet below their route. To get it, someone would have to be let down on a rope. There was no time to linger, for the weather, which changes rapidly in the mountains, was deteriorating. The climbers turned at once to the youngest and smallest

173

member of the party, the twelve-year-old Hans, making his first major climb with his father. It would be easy to let him down. In five minutes they could be on their way again.

"What about it, Hans?" they asked. "Will you do it?"

Hans peered nervously at the narrow ledge with the treasured white flower — and at the sheer drop of hundreds of feet immediately beyond.

"I'll do it," Hans replied, "if my father holds the rope."

It is that attitude of unconditional trust that Jesus is talking about when he says in today's Gospel: "This is the work of God: have faith in the One he sent." The people Jesus was addressing had asked about something else entirely: "What must we do to perform the works of God?" Raised, like many Catholics today, in a tradition that emphasized a long list of commands and prohibitions, they expected Jesus to give them a set of do's and don'ts. Instead he demanded simply faith in the One God had sent.

Still thinking in legalistic terms, the people countered with a request for some authenticating "sign" to justify the faith Jesus was demanding.

> So that we can put faith in you, what sign are you going to perform for us to see? What is the "work" *you* do?

They went on to mention the work Moses had done when, as we heard in the first reading, he had given their ancestors bread from heaven during their desert wanderings.

Gently, Jesus corrected their account of Moses' work. That bread, Jesus explained, had not come from Moses, but from God. The manner in which it was given had itself been a test of faith for those who received it. "Each day the people are to go out and gather their daily portion," God told Moses in to-

174

day's first reading. This, God said, would be a "test, to see whether they follow my instructions or not."

Some of the people had failed that test. Unwilling to trust God, who gave them the food, they disobeyed his command, conveyed through Moses, to gather each day only enough for that day. Some of the people had hoarded the manna — only to find in the morning that it had spoiled (see Exodus 16:16-20). Those people lacked genuine faith. They did not believe that God who fed them today would also provide for their needs tomorrow.

What about ourselves? Do we trust God only when we can see results, when we have proof? Or are we willing to go on trusting when we cannot see, because all is dark and life seems meaningless? That is the kind of faith Jesus asks of us. And faith of that kind is truly, as Jesus says in today's Gospel, "the work of God." It is God's work because it is not something we can produce or demand, through willpower. Nor is it something for which we can take credit. Faith that goes on trusting even when there seems to be no reason for trust is, in the most literal sense, God's work and God's gift.

God bestows this gift on all who ask for it. He may not do so in just the way we want, or at the time we expect. Being willing to leave the manner and the time of this gift to God the giver is itself part of faith, a test of our sincerity in asking for faith. To encourage us to ask for this gift of faith, and to keep on asking, Jesus tells us:

> No one who comes to me shall ever be hungry, no one who believes in me shall thirst again.

What those tremendous words mean is simply this: those who come to Jesus with trusting faith possess something so

175

precious that natural hunger and thirst sink into insignificance.

That is Jesus Christ's personal promise to each one of us. To discover that his promise is true, we must take him at his word. He is inviting us to begin *right now*.

Nineteenth Sunday of the Year

1 Kings 19:4-8; John 6:41-51

"I AM THE BREAD OF LIFE."

• *To help the hearers seek nourishment from both eucharistic tables.*

When we want to explain something new to people, we build on what they already know. Teachers do this with their students, parents with children, industry does it with workers. This is how Jesus taught. He used images which were already familiar to his hearers: the farmer scattering his seed, the shepherd separating sheep from goats, the house built on sand.

Jesus also used familiar expressions from Holy Scripture. Today's Gospel, in which Jesus says, "I am the bread of life," is a case in point. As so often, Jesus took a well-known expression and gave it new meaning.

In the Jewish Scriptures "bread" was often a symbol for spiritual food: the wisdom that God gives to those who approach him in faith and try to do his will. The prophet Isaiah, for instance, portrays God saying to the people (55:1-3):

> Come, you who have no food, buy corn and eat; come and buy, not for money, not for a price. . . . Only listen to me and you will have good food to eat. . . . Come to me and listen to my words, hear me, and you shall have life.

We find another example of this use of bread as a symbol for spiritual food in the prophet Amos. He warns the people that if they persist in disobedience God "will send a famine on the land, not hunger for bread or thirst for water, but for

177

hearing the word of the Lord" (8:11). The book of Sirach also uses bread in this symbolical sense when it says that if a person keeps God's law, wisdom "will nourish him with the bread of understanding and give him the water of learning to drink" (15:3).

When Jesus said, "I am the bread of life," he was building on this foundation, yet giving the symbol of bread deeper meaning. Jesus is himself the divine wisdom that God gives for his people's nourishment. Jesus is the unpurchasable bread of Isaiah. He alone satisfies the hunger and thirst for hearing God's word mentioned by Amos. He is the bread of understanding and the water of learning about which Sirach wrote.

All this wealth of meaning is behind Jesus' simple statement, "I am the bread of life." We Catholics naturally assume that Jesus was referring to the eucharistic bread, and so he was. The Second Vatican Council has reminded us, however, that there are *two* eucharistic tables: the table of the word, and the table of the Lord's body (Liturgy Constitution 48 and 51). We still assume too often that the first part of the Mass, the Liturgy of the Word, is merely a preparation for the "essential" part: consecration and Communion. That is wrong. The Liturgy of the Word is equally important, and equally essential.

Here is what the Council said in 1965 about God's word:

> The church has always venerated the divine Scriptures as she venerates the body of the Lord, in so far as she never ceases, particularly in the sacred liturgy, to partake of the bread of life and to offer it to the faithful from the table of the word of God and the body of Christ.
>
> (Divine Revelation, 21)

178

The Council was saying in that passage that we are nourished not only by the Lord's body and blood in Communion, but equally by hearing God's word. There is a real presence of the Lord in his holy word, as well as in the consecrated bread and wine of the Eucharist. Otherwise the Council could not have spoken of "venerating" the Scriptures just as we venerate the Lord's body.

The Council expanded its teaching about God's word as our spiritual food when it said in the continuation of the same passage:

> In the sacred books the Father who is in heaven comes lovingly to meet his children, and talks with them. And such is the force and power of the word of God that it can serve the church as her support and vigor, and the children of the church as strength for their faith, food for the soul, and a pure and lasting source of spiritual life. Scripture verifies in the most perfect way the words: "The word of God is living and active" (Hebrews 4:12), and "it has power to build you up and give you your heritage among all those who are sanctified" (Acts 20:32; see 1 Thessalonians 2:13).

Today's first reading told how the prophet Elijah journeyed "forty days and forty nights" in the strength of the food God gave him through an angel. In the Gospel Jesus spoke of how God had strengthened the whole people during their wanderings in the desert through manna, or bread, from heaven. Though this bread gave them strength for their journey, it did not make them immortal.

Jesus does not hesitate to claim, however, that the food he gives *does* impart immortality. He says that he is

> the bread that comes down from heaven, for a man to eat and

179

never die. If anyone eats this bread, he shall live forever; the bread I will give is my flesh, for the life of the world.

Jesus means that for those who eat the "living bread" he gives, physical death will be insignificant — only a way station on the journey to eternal life.

Jesus gives himself to us as this "living bread" here in the Eucharist. He does so in two closely linked ways: through his holy word, read and proclaimed in this assembly to God's people; and through his sacramental body and blood, given under the outward forms of bread and wine. Unless we receive the food the Lord offers us at *both* tables, we risk being spiritually undernourished.

When we do partake of both tables, however — by listening devoutly to God's word and by receiving the Lord's body and blood with due preparation and reverence — we can say, in the words of today's responsorial psalm:

Taste and see how good the Lord is;
happy the man who takes refuge in him.

(Psalm 34:9)

Twentieth Sunday of the Year

John 6:51-58

"HOW CAN HE GIVE US HIS FLESH TO EAT?"

• *To help the hearers understand the doctrine of the Real Presence, and its implications for life.*

The words of Jesus that we have just heard mark a turning point in his life in this Gospel according to John. Immediately after this passage, John tells us, "Many of [Jesus'] disciples exclaimed, 'This is more than we can stomach! Why listen to such talk?'" And a few verses later John adds: "From that time on, many of [Jesus'] disciples withdrew and no longer went about with him" (6:60, 66).

What caused this defection? It was Jesus' claim to be himself "the living bread come down from heaven." Jesus' hearers knew all about "bread from heaven." That was the manna with which God had fed his people in the wilderness. That bread had nourished those who received it, but it did not make them immortal. Jesus did not hesitate to claim, however, that if anyone ate the bread *he* would give, that person would "live forever." And he added in explanation: "The bread I will give is my flesh, for the life of the world."

These words caused a violent dispute. Those who were scandalized by Jesus' strong language asked indignantly: "How can he give us his flesh to eat?" The question was understandable. How could a mere man claim that he would give people his flesh to eat and expect to be taken seriously?

Despite the uproar his teaching caused, Jesus did not attempt to soften his claim or explain it away. On the contrary, he strengthened it, speaking now not only about eating his flesh but also about drinking his blood. This was the greatest scandal of all. Jewish law strictly forbade the consumption of blood in any form. Even animal flesh could be eaten only if all the blood had first been drained from it. (See Leviticus 17:10-14; Acts 15:29.)

Jesus also strengthened his previous language about eating his flesh. Up to this point John's original text had used the ordinary Greek word for "eat." After the indignant question, "How can he give us his flesh to eat?" however, John shifts to a stronger word normally used only for the eating of animals — something like "gnaw" or "devour" in English.

Language as strong as that seemed to imply some kind of cannibalism. Small wonder that even many of Jesus' own disciples called his talk "more than we can stomach." No wonder that many "withdrew and no longer went about with him." We might well do the same if the full force of Jesus' teaching, and the magnitude of his claim, had not been dulled for us by constant repetition.

We need to listen afresh to Jesus' words. We need to let them penetrate our hearts, our minds, and souls as if we were hearing them for the first time. Doing so will take us into the heart of our Christian and Catholic faith. For Jesus' words in today's Gospel concern the inner meaning of the Eucharist, in which, as St. Paul tells us, we "proclaim the death of the Lord, until he comes" (1 Corinthians 11:26).

Although John incorporates this teaching about the bread of life into Jesus' long discourse following the miraculous feeding of the crowd in the wilderness, a number of Bible scholars believe that Jesus' words were originally spoken at the Last Supper. To support this view they point out that

182

John gives no account of the institution of the Eucharist. Instead he recounts Jesus' washing of the disciples' feet, and then passes at once to the departure of the traitor, Judas.

Whenever Jesus originally spoke the words, we cannot read them today without reference to the Eucharist. More than the other three Gospels, which record Jesus' institution of the Eucharist, this fourth Gospel, which contains no such record, tells us what the Eucharist does for the believing follower of Christ who participates in this sacred meal with living faith.

The indignant question, "How can he give us his flesh to eat?" is unanswerable apart from faith. If Jesus is a mere man like any other, then clearly he *cannot* give us his flesh to eat. Faith tells us, however, that Jesus, while completely human, is also more than human. He is the one who reveals God. He is God's divine Son.

Physically, the food that Jesus offers us in the Eucharist is ordinary bread and wine. Spiritually, which means in their inner, invisible reality, the consecrated elements are the risen and glorified body and blood of our divine Savior and Lord. Receiving this heavenly food, we become partakers of the divine life that Jesus shares with his heavenly Father and the Holy Spirit. This is why Jesus could say: "The man who feeds on this bread shall live forever." The human life that we received from our parents will not continue forever. The *divine* life, however, given to us first in baptism and nourished in this sacred banquet, *will* continue forever. Because we share in this divine life, Jesus could also say:

He who feeds on my flesh and drinks my blood has life eternal,
and I will raise him up on the last day.

To *benefit* from receiving Christ's body and blood, however,

183

we must come to the Eucharist in living faith: with sorrow for our sins and trust in God's forgiving love. Without such faith we cannot derive nourishment from this spiritual food, any more than our bodies can derive nourishment from ordinary food when our digestion is undermined by illness or unhealthy living. The more faith we bring to the Eucharist, the greater will be its power to bring us close to Jesus Christ and to build up within us his gift of eternal life.

Mindful of the significance of what we do here, and of the great gift that Jesus offers us, listen again to the words of today's responsorial psalm.

> Taste and see the goodness of the Lord.
> I will bless the Lord at all times; his praise shall be ever in my mouth.
> Fear the Lord, you his holy ones, for nought is lacking to those who fear him.
> The great grow poor and hungry; but those who seek the Lord want for no good thing.
> Taste and see the goodness of the Lord.
>
> (34:1, 8-10)

Twenty-first Sunday of the Year

Joshua 24:1-2, 15-17, 18; John 6:60-69

"DECIDE TODAY WHOM YOU WILL SERVE."

• *To challenge the hearers to an unconditioned commitment to Jesus Christ.*

People can be divided into two classes: those who welcome a challenge, and those who avoid challenge because of the risks involved. Two of today's readings are about challenges. In the first reading we heard Joshua, the leader of God's people after the death of Moses, challenge them to renew their unconditioned commitment to the God who had delivered them from bondage in Egypt, and who was about to lead them into a new land. With this new chapter in their national life about to open, Joshua challenged the people to a fundamental decision.

If it does not please you to serve the Lord, decide today whom you *will* serve: the gods your fathers served beyond the River or the gods of the Amorites in whose country you are dwelling. As for me and my household, we will serve the Lord.

The people accepted the challenge. Without hesitation they renewed their unconditioned commitment to serve the true God, whose miraculous care and guidance they had already experienced.

Far be it from us to forsake the Lord for the service of other gods. For it was the Lord, our God, who brought us and our fathers up out of the land of Egypt ... and protected us along our entire journey. ... Therefore we also will serve the Lord, for he is our God.

185

The Gospel records a similar challenge. After recounting Jesus' miraculous feeding of five thousand people in the wilderness, the gospel writer, John, gives us the long discourse on the bread of life. This concludes with Jesus' words: "My flesh is real food. . . . Whoever eats this bread shall live for ever" (6:55, 58).

Offended by the stark realism of this language, many of Jesus' followers turn away from him. Saddened, Jesus addresses the inner circle of the Twelve and challenges them to a decision, very much as Joshua had challenged the people in his day.

"Do you want to leave me too?" Jesus asks. Here, as elsewhere, Peter responds in the name of all: "Lord, to whom shall we go? You have the words of eternal life."

We should not read too much into Peter's words. They do not mean that he and the others have understood Jesus' teaching about giving his flesh as bread for the life of the world. Peter was expressing something deeper: trusting faith — the willingness to embark upon uncharted waters. However hard Jesus' demands, however difficult his teaching, Peter acknowledged a bond that could no longer be broken.

That is the essence of faith: a personal relationship based on trust. The One who asks for this trust challenges us to an *unconditioned commitment*: with no ifs, ands, or buts — with no strings attached. That is hard. For many it is too hard. Challenged to make such a commitment, many people turn away, as the people in today's Gospel turned away from Jesus and "would not remain in his company any longer."

Turning away from the challenge to an unconditioned commitment is called today "keeping your options open." Many people today mistakenly believe that keeping their options open is the key to happiness. That is why many people live to-gether without the commitment of marriage. Others marry with conditions: "as long as we love one another"; "as long as it works out"; "until I find someone better." *Christian* mar-riage means setting no conditions. It means promising faith-fulness to another person "for better, for worse; for richer, for poorer; in sickness, and in health; until death do us part."

The Church asks the same kind of unconditioned commit-ment from candidates for priesthood, from a sister or brother taking religious vows. Who can promise the young man on the day of his priestly ordination, the young woman on the day of her religious profession, that it will work out — not just for five years or for ten, but for a lifetime? No one can make that promise! The commitment must be made simply in faith.

Today, in this hour, the Lord Jesus is challenging you to re-new your commitment to him. If you insist on keeping all your options open, on retaining ultimate control of your life, you may still achieve a measure of fulfillment and happiness. The greatest reward in life, however, you will certainly not achieve. That is reserved for those who dare to make a com-mitment that is unconditioned; whose only option is for the highest and best that they know — for God, as he reveals himself in his Son Jesus Christ.

Right now Jesus Christ is challenging you as his namesake Joshua challenged the people in his day: "Choose today whom you will serve." Will you decide for yourself, for keeping your options open? Or will you decide for Jesus Christ?

He is asking you the same challenging question he put to Peter and those other friends of his: "Will you too go away?"

Happy if you can answer, with Peter: "Lord, to whom shall we go? You have the words of eternal life."

Twenty-second Sunday of the Year

Deuteronomy 4:1-2, 6-8; Mark 7:1-8, 14-15, 21-23

GOD'S LAW.

- *To show the place of God's law in the Christian life.*

Is the most important thing in our religion obeying a set of moral rules? Older Catholics remember a time when this seemed to be true. Today, on the other hand, many Catholics seem to think we can more or less forget about rules as long as our hearts are in the right place.

Two of today's readings are about God's rules. In the first reading Moses warned the people "not to add or subtract" anything from God's holy law. Moreover, Moses made it clear that the Ten Commandments, which embodied God's law, were a privilege and not a burden. In telling his people what he expected of them God had given them more than just directions for their own lives. He had also furnished important clues about his own nature. Other nations lacked such guidance. They had to grope to do God's will in hit-or-miss fashion. Hence the law of the Ten Commandments was a sign of God's special love for the people he had chosen to be his own. The people's acceptance of God's law, and their promise to obey the commandments, were their loving response to the privilege God had bestowed on them.

This view of God's law as a special privilege is central to Jewish religion. It was Jesus' view. Yet in today's Gospel we heard Jesus accuse the religious leaders of his day of perverting God's law. "You disregard God's commandment and cling to what is human tradition." By giving us these two

188

readings today the Church is asking us to reflect on the place of God's law in our lives. Let's take a few minutes to do so.

People can misuse God's law in two ways. One is legal minimalism; the other is maximalism. The minimalizers are always asking: "Do I *have* to?" That is a child's question, not an adult's. Even the tone of voice in which it is generally asked shows its immaturity. Many people go through life asking: "Do I have to?" They pester priests with questions like these:

"Is it a sin, Father?"

"The other priest told me I should, but now things have changed. Do I still have an obligation?"

"Our vacation cabin is forty-seven miles from the nearest Catholic Church. Do we have to go to Mass on Sunday?"

People who pose minimalizing questions like those are really asking how little they can do and still keep on the right side of God. Minimalizers generally know all their minimum obligations by heart. They even know (or think they do) how late they can come to Mass, and how early they can leave, and still have it "count." One thing the minimalizers do not know however: joy. If your first concern is to find out how little you need to give God and his Church, you will experience these minimums not as light, but as heavy burdens. Why is that?

Minimalizers are trying to live with God on the fringe of their lives. They seldom realize that as long as they keep God on the fringe, he will always be a threat to them. He will continually be trying to move into the center. The only people who find joy in their religion are those who live with God *already* at the center of their lives. They have a religion not of law, but of love.

That is how Jesus lived. Like all Jews, Jesus regarded his

people's possession of God's law as a special privilege. God's law was at the heart of Jesus' personal religion. Yet Jesus was no minimalizer. He never worried about fulfilling his minimum obligations. He did that automatically. Jesus never asked: "How little do I *have* to do for God?" He asked instead: "How much *can* I do?" Jesus was like a person in love. No one in love ever asked, when it was a question of doing something for the beloved: "Do I *have* to?" People in love are *glad* to express their love through generosity and self-sacrifice.

The other common misuse of God's law is *maximalism*. Maximalists think they are putting God at the center of their lives. In reality, however, they are as self-centered as the minimalists. By going beyond their minimum obligations they think they can establish a claim that God is bound to honor.

If minimalism is the error of lazy people, maximalism is found most often among pious and religious people. It is sobering to realize that the only people with whom Jesus was severe in the Gospels were the pious and religious.

In today's Gospel, for instance, we heard Jesus use the word "hypocrites" not for notorious sinners, but for people who prided themselves on their exact fulfillment of God's law. Their hyprocrisy lay not in obeying the law but in supposing that this obedience gave them a claim on God. We never have a claim on God. God has a claim on us — and it is an absolute claim. Jesus made this clear when he said: "When you have done all that is commanded of you [and which of us has?] say: 'We are servants and deserve no credit; we have only done our duty' " (Luke 17:10).

God's love and our salvation are not things we can earn. They are God's free gift. God bestows these gifts on us not because *we* are good enough, but because *he* is so good that he

190

wants to share his love with us. God's law is not the list of obligations we must first fulfill before God will love us and bless us. God's law is, rather, the description of our *grateful response* to the love and blessing God bestows on us out of sheer generosity.

Does all this mean that there is no such thing as a "just reward" from God? Of course not. God's reward for faithful service is certain. Jesus tells us this in many passages. He also warns, however, that people who try to calculate their reward in advance risk disappointment. The people who are most richly rewarded — who are literally bowled over by God's generosity — are those who never stop to reckon up their reward because they are so keenly aware of their inner poverty and emptiness.

If we want to experience God's generosity (and is there any one of us who does not?) we must learn to stand before God with empty hands. Then we can experience the joy of Mary, who in her greatest hour, when she learned that she was to be the mother of God's Son, responded with words that climax the daily public prayer of the Church each evening:

"He has filled the hungry with good things, and has sent the rich empty away."

(Luke 1:53)

Twenty-third Sunday of the Year

Isaiah 35:4-7; Mark 7:31-37

"BE OPENED!"

• *To proclaim Jesus as the one who enables us to be open to God, and to one another.*

Total deafness is a terrible handicap. Many people consider it worse than blindness. There are blind people who become accomplished musicians, thinkers, or writers. Blind people are well represented in the learned professions. Deaf mutes, by contrast, seldom have comparable achievements, though they may develop certain skills. Deafness isolates its victims from others far more than blindness. Deaf people see others talking and realize that they are excluded.

The deaf man brought to Jesus by his friends in today's Gospel suffered from this exclusion. Never having heard human speech, the man could speak only indistinctly and with difficulty. Jesus at once took the man apart from the crowd. He had two reasons for doing so.

First, Jesus needed the man's undivided attention. Second, Jesus experienced each act of healing as an intimate encounter with God: something too precious, and too sacred, to be paraded before curious spectators. If Jesus' practice were followed today by all who claim to heal in his name, a number of Sunday television programs would have to go off the air.

Jesus' desire to avoid the reputation of a sensational miracle worker gave him a further reason for forbidding people to publicize his healings. Jesus knew that the one truly important miracle would be the empty tomb. Once in the Gospel according to Mark, therefore, Jesus set a limit to the silence he imposed: when he told the three friends who had witnessed his transfiguration "not to tell anyone what they had seen until the Son of Man had risen from the dead" (9:9). Then the greatest miracle of all, Jesus' resurrection, *could* be proclaimed — as long as the cross was proclaimed with it. Calvary and the empty tomb must never be separated.

What is important about the miracle in today's Gospel, as about all Jesus' healings, is not so much the event itself, as what it tells about the healer. In the first reading we heard Isaiah prophesy that when God's anointed servant, the Messiah, visited the people, "the eyes of the blind will be opened, the ears of the deaf will be cleared . . . the tongue of the dumb will sing."

Jesus' healing of the deaf man fulfilled this prophecy. In an act that spoke more eloquently than words, Jesus was proclaiming that the one so long proclaimed by the prophets had come. In him, Jesus of Nazareth, the carpenter's son, the very power of God was at work. God had visited his people.

Even the details of the healing are significant. Jesus did not tell the man to be patient under his handicap because in heaven his lot would be better. Nor did he urge the deaf man to "offer up" his suffering. How often we hear those two responses to sickness and suffering from those who claim to speak in Jesus' name. We do not hear them, however, from Jesus himself.

Far from accepting the man's deafness, Jesus "emitted a groan" over this fresh example of how suffering had spoiled the beautiful and perfect world God had made. Jesus' heavenly Father and ours is not a God of sickness but of health. We may not assume that any individual sufferer is being punished for personal sin. Yet Scripture clearly teaches that the existence of suffering is connected with man's sin in general (see Genesis 3:16-19; Romans 5:12-14). The man's deafness reminded Jesus of how sin had spoiled his Father's handiwork in creation. That is what caused Jesus to groan.

The heart of the story, however, is Jesus' command to the deaf man: "Be opened!" Deafness had closed the man to others. Jesus wanted to liberate the man from the prison in which his handicap had confined him. Jesus is the man of total openness: openness to God, opennness to those whom society in his day accepted only in subordinate roles, or not at all — children, women, public sinners, and social outcasts. Jesus came, as our fourth eucharistic prayer tells us, "to proclaim freedom to prisoners, the good news of salvation to the poor, and to those in sorrow joy."

Jesus is saying to us what he said to the deaf man: "Be opened!" How closed in we are much of the time: closed to God, closed to others. We shut ourselves up in prisons of our own making, whose walls are self-fulfillment, whose guiding principle is the slogan: "Do your own thing." Most of the conflicts, divisions, and wars in the world — between individuals, families, classes, groups, and nations — are the result of people not being open. In the strife of tongues we hear what we want to hear, and no more; just enough to confirm our prejudices, and then we stop listening altogether. Even between Christians there are barriers erected by our failures to be open to each other. To remedy this un-Christian situation the Second Vatican Council recommended the method of dialogue, which requires us to be open to what the other side is saying — to listen before we speak.

Some conflicts are so grave, however, that no human power

194

seems great enough to break through the walls that separate us from one another. Nor can we penetrate by our own efforts the wall our sins erect between us and God. The Gospel proclaims the good news that there is One who *can* break down these walls. His name is Jesus Christ. Jesus, the man of total openness, has the right, if ever a man had it, to command: "Be opened!" He won that right for all time on Calvary when, in the words of the Church's public prayer,

> For our sake he opened his arms on the cross,
> he put an end to death
> and revealed the resurrection.

(Weekday Preface VI)

Twenty-fourth Sunday of the Year

Mark 8:27-35

"WHOEVER WOULD SAVE HIS LIFE WILL LOSE IT..."

- *To help the hearers surrender more completely to Jesus Christ.*

An airplane flying across an ocean reaches what pilots call "the point of no return." This is the point after which the plane would need more fuel to go back than to continue on. Thereafter the pilot knows that there is no turning around. He must go on.

The Gospel we have just heard showed us Jesus passing *his* point of no return. Previously people had responded to Jesus' message in considerable numbers. Jesus' disciples, though always slow to understand his teaching, were gradually coming to grasp who Jesus was. A conventional success story still seemed possible.

In today's Gospel, however, Jesus faced, and stated "quite openly" (as Mark tells us), that what had once seemed possible was possible no longer. He could no longer expect popular acceptance and success. He could only go forward, knowing that ahead lay rejection, suffering, and death.

Precipitating Jesus' unusually plain statement of the dark future awaiting him, so different from the veiled manner in which Jesus normally spoke about himself, was Peter's confession: "You are the Messiah!" At once Jesus commanded secrecy about his real identity. He wanted to prevent misunderstanding. Everyone assumed that the long awaited Messiah, God's anointed servant, would be the central figure in a glorious success story.

Jesus knew that his disciples shared this view of the Messiah as a national hero who would lead his people to new heights of worldly success. He had to make them realize that this could not be. The future held not triumph but, by all ordinary standards, bitter defeat. This was too much for the disciples to accept. Peter, speaking as so often in the name of all, took Jesus aside to remonstrate with him. Matthew gives us Peter's words: "Heaven preserve you, Lord, this must not happen to you!" (16:22)

Jesus' response to Peter was severe. Calling the man he had chosen as leader of his inner circle "Satan," Jesus told Peter: "You are not judging by God's standards but by man's!" This sharp rebuke shows that Peter's words were a real temptation for Jesus. Passing his point of no return, abandoning the early hopes of success and accepting rejection, suffering, and death — all that cost Jesus an agonizing struggle (see Mark 14:32-36; Hebrews 5:7). Jesus' harsh words to Peter reveal how intense this inner conflict was.

In the passage that follows, addressed to the crowd as well as to the disciples, Jesus made it clear that the road he was traveling would have its parallel in the life of anyone who wished to be his follower. These final words of Jesus in today's Gospel are addressed to us. For most people they are difficult to understand, and even more difficult to follow. Listen to them again in another translation.

Anyone who wishes to be a follower of mine must leave self behind; he must take up his cross, and come with me. Whoever cares for his own safety is lost; but if a man will let himself be lost for my sake and for the gospel, that man is safe.

(New English Bible)

Jesus was talking about far more than what we normally call "self-denial." In telling us that his follower must be willing "to deny his very self," or to "let himself be lost," Jesus meant giving up control of one's destiny. He was talking about accepting weakness, disgrace, suffering, and death, as Jesus himself accepted those things: in the knowledge that those who do "let themselves be lost" in this way are found by God. And not only found: they are taken under God's special and all-powerful protection.

Jesus was talking (to put it another way) about abandoning the attempts we make all the time to retain total control of our lives. Life never really belongs to us in any absolute sense. Life is a gift, entrusted to us for a limited time only. Few of us have a century. Try as we may to keep total control of our destinies, we never quite succeed. At no time do we control our lives completely. At death we lose all control. Most people discover long before that, however, through life's changes and chances, that they are not the masters of their fates and the captains of their souls that we all long to be. Making that discovery can be discouraging. For many it is crushing.

There is One, however, who can "save" our lives for us despite death, indeed through death and beyond. He will do so on the condition, and to the extent, that we surrender control of our lives to him here and now. That is the only way, Jesus tells us in today's Gospel, that we can "preserve" our lives: by turning them over to the One who gave life to us; and who one day will take back his gift, whether we will it or not.

Jesus summons us to do this without anxiety, without fuss, without conditions, and without trying to hold onto a corner of life; but simply surrendering it totally into the hands of the Lifegiver. This act of total self-surrender the Bible calls "faith."

To the extent that we achieve this faith, through surrender to God, we discover the inner meaning of Jesus' life. With that discovery we are able to answer the question that Jesus put to his disciples in today's Gospel, and that he is putting to each one of us right now:

"And you — who do you say that I am?"

Twenty-fifth Sunday of the Year

Mark 9:30-37

"ANYONE WHO WISHES TO RANK FIRST
MUST BE THE SERVANT OF ALL."

• *To encourage the hearers to find Jesus Christ in serving others.*

"What were you discussing on the way?" Jesus asks his disciples in today's Gospel. (The word "home" in our Lectionary version is not in the original.) Mark repeats that phrase "on the way" in the very next sentence and four more times in his Gospel (10:17, 32, 52; 11:8). There was a reason. It was not just any way. Jesus was on the way to Jerusalem where, as he says himself in today's Gospel, "the Son of Man is going to be delivered into the hands of men who will put him to death."

That way was not inevitable. Jesus chose it freely and at great personal cost. The cost grew greater, not smaller, as Jesus approached the end of his self-chosen way. We get a glimpse of the cost in Mark's description of Jesus' agonized prayer in the garden of Gethsemane (14:32-36).

When we are facing difficulties we look for people to help us. Today this may mean joining a "support group." There are support groups for just about everyone these days: for alcoholics and their spouses, for divorced people, single parents, homosexuals, policemen, professionals of all kinds, including priests, for victims of cancer, and other traumatic illnesses. Jesus also had a support group: his Twelve Apostles. One of the reasons he chose them, Mark tells us, was "to be with him" (3:14).

The Twelve did not really give Jesus much support, however.

Those dozen men who accompanied him "on the way" were miles removed from their Master in spirit. While he "set his face resolutely towards Jerusalem" (Luke 9:51), knowing the fate that awaited him there, his closest friends were "arguing about who was the most important." Their behavior illustrates perfectly what Mark has already told us: that these hand-picked friends of Jesus "failed to understand" the ordeal he was facing. This failure, and the resulting inability of the apostles to give Jesus the support he needed, were themselves part of Jesus' suffering. His passion had already begun before he reached Jerusalem, while he was still "on the way."

Today's Gospel shows how Jesus responded: not with a complaint, but with a fresh bid for understanding. Seated — like a rabbi imparting religious teaching to his followers (see Mark 4:1; 13:3) — Jesus told his friends that ordinary standards of importance could not apply for them.

> If anyone wished to rank first, he must remain the last one of all and the servant of all.

This teaching was so crucial for the early Christian community that it was recorded, with variations, four more times in the Gospels (Mark 10:43f, Matthew 18:3f, Luke 9:48; 22:26, John 13:14f).

To drive home his point Jesus placed a small child in their midst and said:

> Whoever welcomes a child such as this for my sake welcomes me . . .

The child does not symbolize innocence (a sentimental modern idea foreign to biblical thought), but *insignificance*. It is as if Jesus were saying to these friends of his: "You are con-

201

cerned with who is most important. If you want to be my disciples, however, you must become, like this child, the *least* important. If you want to find me, look for me in people who are as insignificant as this child, and as easily overlooked."

Jesus' words overturn all normal worldly standards, as prevalent then as now, based on "looking after Number One." Yet Jesus had no interest in promoting a revolution that would sweep away earthly rulers. What Jesus wanted was to create a new way of living that would reflect God's rule, as Jesus reflected it in his own life. God exercises his rule through his merciful love; and Jesus exercises the power he has from his heavenly Father by being the servant of all and at the disposal of all.

Who lives like that today, you ask? More people than you might suppose. Many parents live like that. "Who ever said children brought parents together?" asked the father of three in a parents' support group. To which his wife added: "Since we started having children, my husband and I have had less time for ourselves than we ever thought possible. We can hardly wait for the kids to grow up, so that we can get together again." A recent *Wall Street Journal* article quoted a Catholic bishop in a similar sense: "You can never do what you want to do" was his description of a bishop's life in today's Church.

Would those harrassed parents or the busy bishop exchange their lives with others who have more leisure? They might talk about it. Deep in their hearts, however, they know they would not change even if they could. In their commitment to serving others they are living out Jesus' words: "If anyone wishes to rank first, he must be the servant of all." In putting themselves at the disposal even of those normally considered a nuisance or insignificant, they encounter the One who had time for *everyone*; who was so little concerned with his own importance that he was willing to be "delivered into the hands of men who put him to death"; and who was raised from death the third day, never more to die.

If *you* want to encounter Jesus Christ, look for him in those everyone else ignores. There, in the overlooked, the insignificant, the neediest and most forsaken, he is *waiting* for you.

Twenty-sixth Sunday of the Year

Numbers 11:25-29; Mark 9:38-43, 45, 47-48

DEFENDING THE FAITH?

- *To point out the dangers of frantic orthodoxy.*

A prominent and not entirely happy development in Catholic life today is the growth of something which is best called a "vigilante mentality." We find this in organizations and individuals who are concerned to "defend the faith" against what they like to call "betrayal" and "sellout." The most prominent characteristic of our Catholic vigilantes is not love (which according to the New Testament is the highest virtue), but anger.

The vigilantes are doubtless sincere. Yet in their zeal to defend the faith they overlook the fact that we already have an organization with an excellent record of defending the faith. It is called the Catholic Church. This vigilante mentality is really nothing new. We find it in two of today's readings. In the first reading a young man complained to Moses about irregularities in the church of that day. Two members of God's people were presuming to prophesy — which means to speak for God — without proper authorization. Moses' young aide Joshua, who was slated to be his successor, supported the complaint. Moses rejected it. "Would that all the people of the Lord were prophets!" was Moses' calm reply.

In the Gospel we heard Jesus respond similarly to another zealous defender of the faith: John, the brother of James. Confident that he had acted as Jesus wanted, John reported:

> Teacher, we saw a man using your name to expel demons and we tried to stop him because he is not of our company.

Jesus rebuked his over-zealous disciple, as Moses rebuked a similar case of religious zeal in the first reading.

> Do not try to stop him. No man who performs a miracle using my name can at once speak ill of me. Anyone who is not against us is for us.

Jesus was saying, in effect: "You cannot fence God in. My followers have no monopoly on virtue. There are people who help others simply out of the goodness of their hearts. God will reward them." That is also the significance of Jesus' following words:

> Any man who gives you a drink of water because you belong to Christ will not, I assure you, go without his reward.

The further sayings of Jesus that Mark gives us immediately after these words draw attention to some dangers to the faith which are often overlooked by its over-zealous defenders.

The first, Jesus says, is "leading astray one of these simple believers." By unrestrained attacks on bishops and other pastors, people who today think they are defending the faith actually *undermine* the faith of their fellow Catholics by sowing confusion and doubt. Damage to faith can also come from people who are over-zealous for Church renewal. Introducing even necessary reforms without proper explanation also causes confusion and hurt. This in turn provides a fertile opportunity for self-appointed defenders of the faith to make their charges of "betrayal" and "sellout." Jesus' condemnation of those who undermine others' faith is stern:

> It would be better if [they] were plunged in the sea with a great millstone fastened around their necks.

The Second Vatican Council said in its Constitution on the Church that the Church is "at the same time holy and always in need of being purified" (8). Jesus says the same. Some things need to be changed. Jesus even speaks in today's Gospel of "cutting off" hands, feet, and eyes. He means that our commitment to God must be so total and so radical that we are willing to sacrifice even things as precious as hand, foot, and eye if these things, however good in themselves, stand between us and God.

One example of such pruning in Church life today is the virtual disappearance of the old Latin liturgy. Today's zealous defenders of the faith, citing the Council's directive that "the use of the Latin language is to be preserved" (Constitution on the Liturgy 36,1), charge that its abandonment is the result of a dark "conspiracy" by "enemies of the faith." The truth is both simpler and less dramatic.

History shows that we would almost certainly have had a vernacular liturgy four centuries ago but for the fact that the Protestant reformers of the sixteenth century made the Latin Mass one of the focal points of their attack on the Catholic Church. Thereafter rivers of ink flowed from Catholic pens to defend something which, however beautiful in itself, was never essential to Catholic faith. If it is difficult to find a Latin Mass today, this is because there is so little demand for it. People the world over have found that their own language touches the heart in a way quite impossible for a dead language that few understand well, and most not at all.

The sayings of Jesus collected by Mark in today's Gospel cover a broad field. Yet they are not difficult to summarize.

In rebuking his over-zealous disciple John, Jesus tells us to abandon the vigilante mentality beloved of self-appointed de-

206

fenders of the faith. We are to welcome goodness wherever we find it.

In warning against "leading astray" simple believers, Jesus tells us to show loving consideration even for those whose understanding of faith or whose religious practice differs from our own.

Finally, with his words about cutting off hand, foot, or eye, Jesus summons us to radical and total commitment. He wants us to be willing to sacrifice even things of the highest value when they threaten to come between us and God.

Those are difficult demands. For unaided human nature they are too difficult. That is why we are here: to receive, at these twin tables of God's word and sacrament, the help and strength of him for whom "all things are possible" (Mark 10:27).

Genesis 2:18-24; Hebrews 2:9-11; Mark 10:2-16

GOD'S UNIVERSAL LOVE.

• *To show that God's love embraces all, but especially those whom society treats as inferior.*

The world in which Jesus lived was a man's world. It was a patriarchal society, in which the father was master of his family. A male child was considered more valuable than a female (Leviticus 27:6); and a mother's period of ritual impurity after childbirth was twice as long after the birth of a girl as the birth of a boy (Leviticus 12:1-5).

Women were considered the property of men. A father received a bride-price from the man who married his daughter. She then passed from the control of her father to that of her husband. If he died before she did, his brother, or some other male relative, assumed power over her (Genesis 38:8). The commandment "Thou shalt not covet" lists a man's wife along with his other property (Exodus 20:17; Deuteronomy 5:21). From childhood to old age, the Hebrew woman belonged to the men of her family.

This subordination of women to men was reflected in the Jewish law of divorce, which was available for husbands but not for wives.* In today's Gospel, however, Jesus says that divorce was not part of God's original plan in creation. Divorce

---

*The statement in the Gospel, "The woman who divorces her husband. . ." is not based on Jewish law, which did not permit a wife to divorce her husband. The statement may reflect the situation of Gentile Christians in the Christian community for which Mark wrote.

.

was instituted, Jesus explains, "because of your hard-heartedness" — in other words, as a consequence of sin. It was this hard-heartedness that had created the whole male-dominated world in which Jesus lived. With this world, deformed by sin, Jesus contrasts the good world created by God.

Referring to the Genesis creation story that we heard in the first reading, Jesus says that man and woman were meant to be partners. That first reading opened with God's statement: "It is not good for the man to be alone." The creation of the animals and their naming by the man followed.

Since none of the animals "proved to be the suitable partner" the man needed, God created a partner who was suitable: woman. The man had no part in her creation. God cast him into "a deep sleep" and created the "suitable partner" for man — a phrase connoting woman's equality with man. A number of passages in the Hebrew Scriptures reflect this partnership between the sexes intended by God in creation (Hosea 2:16; Jeremiah 31:22; Song of Songs, *passim*). Genesis also makes it clear that the domination of women by men was a consequence of sin (3:16).

In the Gospel Jesus strongly affirms this partnership between the sexes intended by God in creation, and hence the fundamental equality of man and woman. His teaching about marriage and divorce is a strong condemnation of the double standard which prevailed in his world: a strict law for women, and a more indulgent one for men. If men and women are partners, equally loved by God, there can be only one standard for both.

The passage that follows, in which Jesus welcomes little children and blesses them, makes the same point. We are all God's children, all equally dear to him. The same social and legal system that assigned women a lower place than men also considered children inferior. Girls were inferior because of their sex. And even boys below the age of twelve were considered to be incomplete persons: unable to fulfill all the provisions of the law, and hence incapable of good works.

This explains why Jesus' disciples thought they were doing him a favor by keeping children away from him. Jesus rejected their treatment of children, however, as he had already rejected the treatment of women in his world.

> Let the children come to me and do not hinder them. It is to just such as these that the kingdom of God belongs.

Jesus' point is that God's kingdom is especially for those whom society considers of no importance: people who are overlooked, thrust aside, pushed around, imposed on. Hence the importance of women to Jesus, and of children.

Behind *both* parts of the Gospel — the seemingly legalistic teaching about marriage and divorce, and the scene of Jesus with little children — is the message of *God's universal love*. The world of man's marring has perverted this love into lust, which means using others for selfish pleasure. Instead of partnership between the sexes, there is rivalry: domination on the one hand, manipulation on the other.

We pervert God's universal love also when instead of welcoming children as God's gift, we resent them as burdens that interfere with our comfort. This is the attitude that has produced, in country after country, laws permitting the killing of unborn children, often for the most trivial of reasons — in many cases simply because their birth might be an inconvenience. Already we are witnessing the next logical development: the direct killing of the newborn, mostly through starvation, when they have some physical or mental handicap.

In the face of these and countless other horrors, the Church proclaims Jesus' timeless message of God's universal love for all whom he has made — not just for people of "good moral character," but for all. In a special way, Jesus tells us, God loves the weak, the defenseless, the neglected. He loves every one of us just as we are, in strength and weakness. He calls us to place great value on ourselves, and on one another.

God did not make us for rivalry, for exploitation, for strife and war. God made us to support one another. He made us to be partners. He made us for love. In the world of God's making that love was as natural as breathing. In the world of our marring, the power to love must be given us afresh, from outside. The One who gives us this love is the one who *is* love himself. He is the one, our second reading tells us, who is "not ashamed" to call us — every one of us — his brothers and sisters.

His name is Jesus Christ.

Twenty-eighth Sunday of the Year

Mark 10:17-30

"WITH GOD ALL THINGS ARE POSSIBLE."

• *To show that all things are possible for the person who trusts completely and solely in God.*

"How much money is enough?" a famous millionaire was asked once. Unhesitatingly the man replied: "Always just a little more." Even millionaires would like "just a little more." There are few rich people who do not know someone even wealthier than they are. This enables even millionaires to think of themselves as not "really" rich.

If that is true even of millionaires, where does that leave the rest of us? It is all too easy for us to dismiss the story in today's Gospel about the rich man who asked Jesus what he must do to inherit eternal life. The story is not for us, we feel. We can safely ignore it.

In fact we dare not ignore the story. It takes us into the heart of the Gospel. It is not really about riches at all, or at least only incidentally. And insofar as the story does have to do with wealth, it concerns not just money but other forms of riches that are far more common.

Far from being different from us, the rich man who comes to Jesus with his question about salvation closely resembles us. He is a faithful, devout churchgoer who has made since childhood a sincere and generous effort to keep all the rules of his religion. Even the way he approaches Jesus shows how religious the man is. Like a devout Catholic of an earlier day genuflecting to kiss the bishop's ring, the man kneels before

212

Jesus in reverence. Not content with the normal salutation, "Rabbi — Teacher," the man addresses Jesus as "*Good* Teacher." In correcting him, Jesus was not denying his own goodness but reminding the man that even the greatest human virtue is only a pale reflection of God's goodness.

Unless we see how generous the man was, we miss the whole point of the story. He really had kept all the rules, all his life: "since childhood," he tells Jesus. Which one of us could say the same? How devastated the man must have been, then, to hear Jesus tell him he must still do "one thing more." When the man heard what it was, he was crushed. "Sell *everything?*" we can imagine him asking in shocked disbelief. "You've got to be kidding!" No wonder that "his face fell," that "he went away sad." Wouldn't you? After all, enough is enough.

Jesus' disciples were equally shocked. Their religion taught them that wealth was a sign of God's favor. And now Jesus had just said that riches excluded people from God's kingdom. No wonder the disciples were "completely overwhelmed" and wanted to know: "Who then can be saved?" The question has only one possible answer. If entrance into God's kingdom is reserved for those who, in addition to keeping all the rules of their lives, give away everything they own, then *no one* is in heaven, not even the Blessed Mother herself! She might make it on the basis of keeping all the rules. Yet she presumably had a house and few possessions, however modest. So she would be excluded on that score at least.

Jesus confirmed the impossibility of getting to heaven by our own efforts when he announced flatly: "With man it is impossible." Yet he added at once: "But not for God: with God *all things are possible*."

What Jesus was saying is simply this. "If you think you can get to heaven by your own efforts, forget it. You cannot. It is impossible. Even keeping all the rules wouldn't get you in, supposing you had kept them all — which you haven't. Paying me all kinds of compliments and showing reverence won't admit you either. Heaven is not the result of anything you do or ever can do. Heaven is the result of what *God* does — *for* you. Getting into heaven is a *miracle*, a miracle of grace. Heaven is *God's free gift*."

Jesus did not tell the man to sell all he had because riches were evil. Rightly used, wealth is good. Riches become a danger for us, however, whenever they give us a false sense of security. Money does this, but other things as well. Jesus mentions some of them in today's Gospel: family, parents, children, property. Even our *good works* can give us a false sense of security by misleading us into thinking they give us a claim on God. Not all the prayers and virtues and sacrifices in the world give us a claim on God. God has a claim on *us*, and it is an absolute claim.

Jesus summons us, as he summoned the rich man in today's Gospel, to trust in God and in him alone. He wants us to see that true discipleship goes beyond keeping a set of rules and believing a list of truths. The demands Jesus makes on us *are* impossible. We need to get that straight from the start. They are impossible, that is, for everyone *except God*. "For God all things are possible." That sentence from today's Gospel runs like a golden thread throughout Holy Scripture. It was God's message to Abraham (Genesis 18:14), to Mary (Luke 1:37), to the rich man in today's Gospel. It is God's message to each one of us today.

When life is too much for you; when you are weighed down

by anxiety, illness, injustice, the claims of others, or the nagging sense of your own inadequacy; when God's demands on you seem too great — whenever, in short, you come up against *the impossible*; then you are up against God. He is the God of the impossible. In every impossible situation, in every trial that is too hard for you to bear, his divine Son and your best friend is saying to you, with tender love:

For you it is impossible but not for God. With God all things are possible!

Twenty-ninth Sunday of the Year

Mark 10:35-45

"THE GREATEST AMONG YOU
   SHALL BE THE SERVANT OF ALL."

* *To apply Jesus' teaching about serving others to Church life today.*

Jesus' disciples were remarkably slow to grasp the significance of his life and teaching. Today's Gospel is a good example. The two brothers, John and James, come to Jesus with an important request. "See to it that we sit, one at your right and the other at your left, when you come into your glory."

The misunderstanding was in those two words: "your glory." Jesus' glory would be radically different from anything those two friends of his expected. No wonder Jesus responded: "You do not know what you are asking." At once he challenged them with the counter-question: "Can you drink the cup I shall drink or be baptized in the same bath as I?"*

Lightheartedly Jesus' two friends replied: "We can." Clearly they had still not understood what lay ahead for the Master whom they so revered. The "cup" Jesus referred to would be a cup of bitter suffering. His "baptism" would not be in water but in blood. If his friends had really understood that, they might not have been so eager to share in his "glory," as they so lightly termed it.

The indignation of the other disciples upon learning of this

---

*The words "of pain" in the Lectionary translation are not in the original.

exchange continued the misunderstanding. They were resentful that two of their number seemed to be taking unfair advantage by claiming the places of honor in Jesus' kingdom before any of them. Patiently Jesus explained that this whole contest for places of honor was totally unacceptable among his followers. God's kingdom was not what they supposed it to be or wanted it to be. God's kingdom would come in his way only, not in theirs. And God's way was radically different from man's.

It is easy to feel superior to the disciples. Yet are we really any better at understanding Jesus' message? "God helps those who help themselves," we say. Too often "helping ourselves" takes the form of "looking after Number One." Any number of popular self-help books tell us how to do this. Such books enjoy enormous sales.

Young people today are sometimes called "The Me Generation." This description fits many who are no longer young by any standard. From childhood to old age our society emphasizes convenience and comfort. At the slightest inconvenience we are prone to think our "rights" are being violated. Every day the media report about people protesting the supposed infringement of their rights.

For every right, however, there is a corresponding duty. We all know how popular the concept of duty is today. Too often duties are what we think others owe to us, not what we owe to those with whom we live, or to society as a whole. We want what we want when we want it. What else is this but the scramble for position, for power, for the influence that Jesus condemns in today's Gospel?

This competition for power and influence is widespread in the Church. We clergy see examples of it every day. The devil ruins some of our most promising and gifted priests through ambition. It is no secret that in a celibate clergy ambition is the clerical form of lust.

Today, however, lay people are also involved in this un-Christian power struggle. We see this, for instance, in the argument over whether parish councils are decision-making bodies or "merely consultative." One of the best comments on this debate was made by the founding pastor of a new parish who said that if his parish council could not make decisions he saw little point in having it. He added that although he had the power to veto any council decision, in ten years he had never used this right. (See Robert D. Fuller, *Adventures of a Collegial Parish*, p. 37; Twenty-Third Publications, Mystic, Conn., 1981.) Such a record is a tribute to all concerned.

The parish council is a practical expression of the teaching of the Second Vatican Council that

> if by the will of Christ some are made teachers, pastors, and dispensers of mysteries on behalf of others, yet all share a true equality with regard to the dignity and to the activity common to all the faithful for the building up of the body of Christ.
>
> (Constitution on the Church, 32)

Rightly used, the parish council is a means for arriving at *consensus* and so building up the *unity* of God's people. When, on the other hand, the council becomes an arena in which pastor and people confront each other in an atmosphere of mistrust and hostility, those responsible for this situation are violating the fundamental law laid down by Jesus in today's Gospel for his followers:

> It cannot be like that with you. Anyone among you who aspires

to greatness must serve the rest; whoever wants to rank first among you must serve the needs of all.

Here in the Eucharist Jesus reinforces these words with his example. Here he offers us not merely his body, but his *broken* body, and his *poured out* blood. The price of these gifts was the Lord's death. In his Second Letter to the Corinthians (5:15-17), Paul states the reasons for Christ's death thus:

His purpose in dying for all was that men, while still in life, should cease to live for themselves, and should live for him who for their sake died and was raised to life. With us, therefore, worldly standards have ceased to count . . . When anyone is united to Christ, there is a new world, the old order has gone, and a new order has already begun.

Of that new order and that new world we are citizens. The first citizen of all is "the Son of Man [who] came not to be served but to serve — to give his life in ransom for the many." He summons us to follow where he has led, and to imitate his example.

Thirtieth Sunday of the Year

Mark 10:46-52

"GET UP! HE IS CALLING YOU!"

- *To challenge the hearers to deeper conversion.*

Suppose a journalist from Russia or China were to ask whether there was much begging in the United States. Any one of us would answer with an indignant "No." We associate begging with poor, Third World countries, not with this "land of the free and home of the brave."

In fact, there are more beggars in our midst than most people realize. A priest walking down skid row is almost sure to be asked for money for a cup of coffee from at least one pathetic figure clearly suffering from the effects of a stronger brew. Near bus terminals the request is often for a ticket to a distant city, where a job is waiting to relieve the petitioner from his temporary financial embarrassment.

In every major air terminal in the country neatly turned out young people, "in the exercise of their constitutional rights" (as the airport signs inform us), use all kinds of tricks to inveigle the unwary into conversation. According to the carefully rehearsed scenario this is supposed to end only when the embarrassed traveler parts with five or preferably ten dollars to avoid further harassment. Seldom are donors informed that they have just contributed to the religious sect called Hare Krishna.

Harassment was the stock-in-trade of the blind beggar Bartimaeus in today's Gospel. He would sit by the roadside in a pathetic heap crying out his mournful litany to passersby whom he could hear but not see. Bartimaeus is at his accustomed station early today. He has heard that the famous rabbi Jesus of Nazareth is coming to town. There will surely be a big turnout for a celebrity of this importance. With any luck Bartimaeus should have a good day.

From a distance Bartimaeus hears the sound of an approaching crowd. They are chanting one of the psalms used by pilgrims on their way to Jerusalem. Surely this must be the rabbi himself, on the way to the holy city for Passover.

At once Bartimaeus starts to cry out the flattering salutation which he has rehearsed in advance: "Jesus, Son of David, have pity on me!" Annoyed that this squalid town beggar should disturb the famous rabbi's pilgrimage, the bystanders tell Bartimaeus to be quiet. He pays no attention. This is his big opportunity. He continues to cry out at the top of his voice.

Though Bartimaeus cannot see it, Jesus has stopped. He is telling his friends to summon the man whose voice he can still hear through the crowd. "Get up!" the people tell Bartimaeus. "He is calling you!" Overjoyed at this unexpected good fortune, Bartimaeus jumps to his feet, throwing aside as he does so the tattered cloak which he uses to enhance the impression of pathetic misery.

"What do you want me to do for you?" Jesus asks when the blind man stands before him. Bartimaeus never expected anything like this. "Rabbi," he hears himself saying, "I want to see." The words which follow in Mark's account are the most important in the whole story.

> Immediately he received his sight and started to follow [Jesus] *on the way.*

221

To follow Jesus "on the way" has a special, spiritual significance in this Gospel according to Mark. It was no ordinary way. The way Jesus was walking would take him to Jerusalem, the site of his passion, death, and resurrection. When Mark wrote that Bartimaeus started to follow Jesus on that way, therefore, he meant that Bartimaeus had become Jesus' disciple. The fact that this man, alone of all the people Jesus healed in this Gospel, is *named*, indicates that he was probably well known to the Christian community for which Mark wrote. He was one of them.

That encounter on the way outside Jericho shortly before Passover had changed Bartimaeus' life. He had gone there looking for money. He found something far better than even the most generous benefactor could give: not only the restoration of his physical sight, but *spiritual* vision as well to recognize Jesus — to see that following Jesus was the best thing he could do with his life.

Into this simple story of the healing of a blind beggar Mark has compressed the whole process of Christian conversion. It begins, seemingly, with Bartimaeus' search for money. In reality, however, God was already searching for *him*. He had already sent his Son, Jesus of Nazareth, to call Bartimaeus. Jesus' call reached him not directly, but through others. Those messengers challenged Bartimaeus to act. "Get up! He is calling you!"

Even after Bartimaeus responded to this call, however, he still needed others to lead him to Jesus. Through his encounter with Jesus Bartimaeus discovered something far better than the money he had been looking for. He found the one whose companionship meant everything to him. He decided to follow Jesus "on the way" — to become his disciple.

This is the way God calls each one of us. He uses other people to extend the call of his Son to those who are bogged down in the quest for things of temporary value. The messengers who extend the call assist those who respond to find Jesus. In the encounter with him they find their lives changed. Jesus gives them new inner, spiritual vision. They discover new values — the values of the one friend in all creation for whom, and with whom, life is truly worth living.

"Get up! He is calling you!" That is Jesus' message to each one of us. It is his message to *you*! Have you heard the message? Have you responded to it? Are you passing the message on to others? If not, what *are* you passing on? Whether you know it or not, your life is making a *statement*. Is it a statement *for* Jesus Christ — or against him?

If you are uncertain what statement your life is making, you need to listen again to the call. Jesus *is* calling you. The farther you are from him, the more urgently he is calling to you. You need to do what Bartimaeus did: to get up, to cast aside the things that hinder you, to come to Jesus. He wants to heal you of your inner, spiritual blindness. He wants you to follow him "on the way."

Thirty-first Sunday of the Year

Deuteronomy 6:2-6; Mark 12:28-34

THE GREATEST COMMANDMENT.

• *To show that God's law embodies his love; and that our obedience to the law is our response to that love.*

At the heart of Jesus' religion were the Ten Commandments given by God to Moses. From these the rabbis had developed by Jesus' day a list of 613 separate laws: 248 commands and 365 prohibitions. Obviously no one could possibly remember all those laws in daily life, any more than Catholics today can remember all 1752 laws in our Code of Canon Law. Hence the rabbis vied with each other to formulate a "greatest" or most important law that would sum up everything God commanded.

One of the most famous of these attempts was that of the Rabbi Hillel, a contemporary of Jesus, who undertook to summarize the whole law while standing on one foot. "What you yourself hate, do not to your neighbor," Rabbi Hillel said. "That is the whole of God's law. Everything else is commentary."

This quest for a summary of the law was behind the question put to Jesus in today's Gospel about the "first of all the commandments." In reply Jesus cited the passage from Deuteronomy which we heard in our first reading. This is the celebrated Hebrew formula "Shemáh Israél — Hear, O Israel," recited to this day by devout Jews thrice daily. Two things are noteworthy about this central text of Jewish religion.

First, it presents what we owe God as a *response* to what

God has already done for us. The first phrase, "The Lord our God is Lord alone," reflects the special relationship between God and his people. "This *one* God," the text is saying, "is *our* God because he has chosen *us* from all other nations on earth to be his own." The duty to love God is the *consequence* of God's prior choice of this people. "The Lord our God is Lord alone! *Therefore* you shall love the Lord your God. . ."

This view of the law as man's response to God's prior action is even clearer in the Ten Commandments. They are preceded by the words: "I am the Lord your God who brought you out of Egypt, out of the land of slavery" (Exodus 20:2; Deuteronomy 5:6). The commandments that follow describe the grateful response of God's people to what God has already done for them in rescuing them from bondage.

The Deuteronomy text cited by Jesus in the Gospel is noteworthy for a second reason as well. It puts *love* at the heart of religion. We sometimes hear that the Old Testament presents a God of wrath, and the New Testament a God of love. That is untrue. The Old Testament presents a God of *law*. Yet God's law is *an expression of his love*, a sign of his special favor granted to his own people, and not to others (see Deuteronomy 4:6-8).

The New Testament does present a God of love. Yet he remains a God of law. Jesus said that he came not to abolish the law but to fulfill it (Matthew 5:17). And he gave "a new commandment: love one another" (John 13:34). *Both* parts of the Bible disclose the *same* God. If God's self-disclosure is fuller in the New Testament, this is because in it God comes to us through his Son (see Hebrews 1:1f).

The rabbis who compiled from the Ten Commandments the list of 613 separate laws also taught that they were so closely linked that disobeying one was equivalent to disobeying all. There is an echo of this teaching in the Sermon on the Mount, where Jesus says: "If anyone sets aside even the least of the Law's demands . . . he will have the lowest place in the kingdom of heaven" (Matthew 5:19). By making *love* the center of God's law, however, Jesus clearly moved beyond this tradition. Love of God and of neighbor is the heart of Jesus' own summary of the law in today's Gospel. When his questioner affirmed that love was better even than formal worship, Jesus told him: "You are not far from the reign of God." With these words Jesus was saying that God's reign is present wherever true love is present.

How can we tell when this true love which is the heart of God's law is present? Jesus' answer is clear. The test of our love for God is *whether we love our neighbor* (see Matthew 25:40, 45; 1 John 4:20). And love for our neighbor is a matter of deeds, not feelings. If it means sharing with others the unmerited love that God lavishes on us. This is the love for neighbor that God commands in his law.

Human laws command us to respect our neighbors' rights. Obedience to such laws, however, is always impersonal, formal, cold. If I merely respect your rights, there is no true human contract between us. Hence the enormous amount of *loneliness* in our society. Mother Teresa calls loneliness "the worst disease of modern times."

There is only one cure for loneliness: love. And the source of all love is God, for "God *is* love" (1 John 4:9). God's law can command this love, as human laws cannot, because at the heart of God's law is the world's greatest love: the love of God for all that he has made.

We often experience conflict between love for God and love

for neighbor. According to Jesus, however, there *is* no conflict. Love for neighbor is the expression and test of our love for God. "Insofar as you did it to one of the least of these brothers of mine," Jesus says in his great parable of judgment, "you did it *to me*" (Matthew 25:40).

Our world is full of schemes for serving people in need. In many western countries they are called the welfare state; elsewhere we speak of socialism or communism. Why do these efforts so often leave people still hungry, hurt, and lonely? Because they are not empowered by the love of God! All forms of do-goodism without love are cold. They end by exploiting those they wish to serve and depriving them of their human dignity and freedom. *There* is the explanation for the ghastly failure of so many ambitious and well intentioned schemes for human betterment in our world.

For all these failures despite the enormous amount of goodwill involved there is but one remedy: the unbounded love of God — the love which is a free gift, not a reward for services rendered; the love that will never let us go. We are here to receive that gift. The One who gives us his love as a gift sends us out, to *share* his gift with others.

Thirty-second Sunday of the Year

Mark 12:38-44

SACRIFICING ALL, TO RECEIVE ALL.

• *Through the example of the widow's generosity to motivate the hearers to deeper faith.*

The temple in Jerusalem in Jesus' day was divided into a number of different areas to which access was increasingly restricted. Outside was the Court of the Gentiles. This was open to all. The first area inside was the Women's Court, open only to Jews. The Men's Court admitted only Jewish males. The Court of the Priests was for them alone. Finally came the most sacred area of all: the Holy of Holies, which could be entered only by the High Priest, and by him only once a year.

Around the walls of the Women's Court were thirteen urns shaped like trumpets for the receipt of the temple tax and other offerings. Visitors to the temple did not place their contributions in these receptacles themselves, however. They gave them to the priest on duty, mentioning the amount and what it was for. The priest then announced the offering and deposited it in the appropriate urn.

This explains how Jesus could know the amount given by the poor widow in today's Gospel. The commentators believe she wanted to make an "unrestricted gift." As such it would have been placed in the thirteenth urn, the receipts of which were used to purchase animals for the temple sacrifices. Her gift did not benefit the poor or some other "good cause." It was for the sole honor of God.

Such a gift, especially from a woman who was herself poor,

was sure to provoke criticism. The Gospels record this criticism in the case of the woman who anointed Jesus' feet with costly perfume. "Why this waste?" some of the bystanders said angrily on that occasion. The perfume could have been sold for a handsome sum, they protested, and the money given to the poor. (See Mark 14:5.)

This criticism will always be heard whenever people offer gifts for the sole honor of God. Such gifts can never be justified in purely this-worldly, utilitarian terms. They can be justified only on the basis of *faith*. And for those with faith, no justification is necessary.

Faith alone can explain the widow's gift. Faith alone can motivate such a gift. That is what Jesus emphasized in his comment. The utilitarian, worldly view sees the woman's action as, at best, insignificant (What good is so trifling a gift?); at worst a scandal — that a woman so poor herself should give all she had to live on, and not even for a "good cause" at that, but simply to be wasted for God.

Jesus saw her action from the perspective of faith, which is the perspective of God. God looks not at the outward action nor at appearances. God looks at the heart. In God's eyes what counts, therefore, is not the size of the gift but its *motive*. The wealthy contributors were motivated at least in part by the desire for human recognition and praise. The widow could hope for no such recognition. Her gift was too insignificant to be noticed. For God, however, no gift is too small provided it is made in the spirit of total self-giving that comes of faith and is nourished by faith.

Jesus recognized this total generosity in the widow. She gave all she had to live on for that day. Even the detail that her gift consisted of two coins is significant. She could easily have kept one for herself. Human prudence would say that she should have done so. She refused to act out of prudence. She wanted to give totally, disregarding prudence, trusting in God alone.

Jesus was referring to the totality of the widow's gift when he said that she had given "more than all the others." They *calculated* how much they could afford to give. In the widow's case such calculation could lead to only one conclusion: She could not afford to give anything! Her poverty excused her from giving at all. She refused to calculate. She preferred instead to trust in him for whom "all things are possible" (Mark 9:23; 10:27; 14:36).

Mark's choice of this little incident to conclude his account of Jesus' public ministry is another example of the artistry with which he has composed this seemingly simple Gospel. Immediately following this story Mark gives us Jesus' teaching about "the last days." He then moves swiftly to the Passover, Last Supper, and Crucifixion. In saying that this poor widow "gave all that she had," Jesus was anticipating his own total self-giving, soon to be consummated on Calvary. There he would give all *he* had, even life itself.

This poor widow, known to us by this single act and not even by name, shows us better than long theoretical explanations what it means to be a follower of Jesus Christ. True Christian discipleship will always seem foolish, even mad, to those who live by worldly wisdom. This widow lived by a higher wisdom, the wisdom of faith. With her small gift she took her place alongside the other great biblical heroes of faith, from Abraham to Mary, who set their minds first on God's kingdom, confident that their daily necessities would be provided by him who (as Jesus says) "knows that you have need of these things" (Luke 12:30). She is one of those Jesus was speaking of when he said: "Fear not, little flock; for your Father has chosen to give you the kingdom" (Luke 12:32).

This poor widow is one of that "huge crowd which no one can count" (Revelation 7:9) that we thought of recently on All Saints' Day — those who out of faith sacrificed all for Jesus Christ and in so doing received from him the "hundredfold reward" that he promised (Mark 10:30).

Now, in this hour, Jesus is inviting each one of us to join that happy company: to sacrifice all, that we may receive all. Why not begin — *today*?

Thirty-third Sunday of the Year

Hebrews 10:11-14, 18

"ONE SACRIFICE FOR SINS FOREVER."

• *To explain the doctrine of eucharistic sacrifice and its signifi-cance for us today.*

Mother Teresa says that "the worst disease in the world today is loneliness." The longing to give one's self in love, and to know that one is loved in return, is as universal as life itself. This longing is behind the familiar sentence in the Genesis story (2:18):

> Then the Lord God said, "It is not good for the man to be alone. I will make a partner for him."

We seek the fulfillment for which our hearts long in friend-ship and marriage. And beyond these human relationships people from the beginning of time have sought a remedy for the deepest longings of their hearts, and their inner empti-ness, through fellowship with God.

The search for fellowship with God has often taken the form of offering God *sacrifice*. The purpose of the sacrifice may be to atone for sin, to show gratitude for blessings re-ceived, or to reinforce the prayer for future favors. Sacrifice may also take the form of a religious meal through which the worshipers seek to enter into communion with God. Jesus' re-ligion permitted sacrifice only in the temple at Jerusalem, which was thought to be the dwelling place of God on earth.

Increasingly, however, Jesus' people came to realize that there was a fundamental flaw in the sacrifices they offered to God: God did not need or want material things, since he was the creator of everything anyway, and hence their true owner. God was interested not so much in *gifts* as in the *giver*. Yet this was the one thing people could not offer to God in sacrifice. And to the extent that people did try to offer themselves to God, their offerings were tainted by sin and hence unworthy of God, who deserved a *perfect* offering.

The realization that the sacrifices offered in the Jerusalem temple never *really* made up for human sin lies behind the opening sentence of today's second reading:

> Every priest [and the author is referring to *Jewish* priests in the Jerusalem temple] stands ministering day by day, and offering again and again those same sacrifices *which can never take away sins.*

It is part of the good news that Jesus came to proclaim that this failure at the heart of his people's religion has been ended. A perfect sacrifice *has* been offered to God once: one truly worthy of him, one that does make up for and take away the guilt of all sins for all time. This perfect sacrifice has actually achieved what all previous offerings tried to achieve without success. It has put an end to human isolation and loneliness by bringing us into loving fellowship with the one who alone can satisfy the deepest longings of our hearts: God himself.

This perfect sacrifice was offered by Jesus Christ. It began with his birth in obscurity in a remote village on the edge of the then-known world. It continued through the whole of Jesus' life, which he lived always in perfect obedience to his Father's will. Jesus completed this offering of his sinless life to his Father on Calvary with the words: "It is consummated" (John 19:30).

Our second reading is referring to this self-offering of Jesus Christ when it contrasts the repeated offering of material sacrifices in the Jerusalem temple, "which can never take away sins," with the perfect sacrifice of Jesus Christ.

But Jesus offered one sacrifice for sins and took his seat forever at the right hand of God . . . By one offering he has forever perfected those who are being sanctified. Once sins have been forgiven, *there is no further offering for sin.*

That last phrase arrests our attention at once. It seems to contradict the Church's teaching that there *is* a daily repeated offering for sin: the Eucharist. We are confronted with a dilemma. *Either* Jesus' self-offering, consummated on Calvary, was truly all-sufficient, unique and unrepeatable — in which case it is difficult to see how we can say that the Mass is a sacrifice. *Or* the Mass *is* a sacrifice — in which case Jesus' sacrifice on Calvary was *not* all-sufficient. To resolve this dilemma we must ask: what is the relationship between the Mass and Calvary?

To answer that question we need to go behind Calvary to the Last Supper. There Jesus used the familiar symbolism of the Jewish Passover meal to interpret for his friends what he was about to do the next day. Giving thanks to God over bread and wine, which is the Jewish way of blessing them, Jesus said: "This is my body . . . This is my blood." But he said more. He called the bread "my body *given for you.*" The wine he called "my blood *poured out for you.*" That is Jewish sacrifice language. Jesus was referring to the sacrifice of his body and blood on Calvary, where his body would be broken and his blood poured out.

Finally, Jesus gave his friends a *command*: "Do this in my

memory." When, in obedience to that command, we "do this," both Jesus himself, and his sacrificial self-offering to the Father, are truly present with us. Here in the Eucharist we have not merely Jesus' body and blood, under the outward forms of bread and wine. Here we have Jesus' *broken* body, and his *poured out* blood.

Jesus' sacrifice is not repeated. Rather it is *made present*. As Jesus presented his sacrifice "ahead of time," as it were, at the Last Supper, so his unrepeatable, unique, all-sufficient sacrifice offered once for all on Calvary is again presented and made present each time we obey Jesus' command to "do this" in his memory.

The Mass is not just a mental recalling of Jesus' action at the Last Supper and Calvary. Here our crucified and risen Lord is truly present. Spiritually, which means invisibly but truly, the unique and unrepeatable past event of the Last Supper and Calvary is made present as we celebrate that event in sacred signs. Those signs, bread and wine, make present *both* him whom they signify *and* his action for us. Here time and space fall away. Here we are able to stand with Mary and the Beloved Disciple at the cross, with but one exception: we cannot see Jesus with our bodily eyes, only with the eyes of faith.

There is yet another dimension to the Mass. Because Jesus has offered the one perfect sacrifice acceptable to God, the offerings we make to him are no longer unacceptable, despite our sins. Offered together with Jesus' sacrifice (which is here commemorated, celebrated and made present, though not repeated), our offering of ourselves, our souls and bodies *is* accepted by God. What we offer to God is imperfect, because we are imperfect. Yet offered together with Christ's perfect sac-

235

rifice, our littleness is swallowed up in his greatness. Our imperfection is covered over by Christ's perfection.

Mindful of the true significance of what we do here, I invite you to supply for once the ending to the sermon, as we say with fresh understanding the words the Church gives us to say at every Mass:

Pray, brethren, that our sacrifice may be acceptable to God the Almighty Father.
(*Response*): May the Lord accept the sacrifice at your hands
for the praise and glory of his name,
for our good, and the good of all his church.

Christ the King

Revelation 1:5-8; John 18:33-37

CHRIST'S KINGSHIP — AND OURS.

- *To proclaim the redemptive power of Christ's unconditioned love, and the privileges and obligations he lays upon us.*

Pilate's question was simple: "Are you a king?" He was exasperated when the prisoner before him refused to give a straight yes-or-no answer. Jesus seldom gave people the clear and simple answers they wanted. In this case Jesus could not answer "No," for he was a king. Yet if he answered "Yes," he was sure to be misunderstood, for his kingship was totally different from all others. Jesus is a king whose rule was inaugurated not in glory but in suffering.

Today's second reading gives us further information about Jesus' kingship. It calls him the greatest of all kings: "ruler of the kings of earth." The words that follow tell us three things that this greatest of all kings has done for us.

1. *He loves us.*

Do we really think of Jesus Christ as the representative and Son of a *loving* God? Or do we think of God as angry, or at least as some kind of stern judge who is just waiting for us to break one of his many rules? If we do think of God as someone who loves us, don't we often assume that his love has strings attached? that God will love us only if we keep his rules and thus demonstrate that we are *worthy* of his love?

To conceive of God as an angry deity or a stern judge is a radical denial of the Gospel proclaimed by his Son. So is the idea that God's love is conditional on our good behavior. "Gospel" means "good news." Is it good news to be told that

God is vengeful, or that he will not love us unless we first earn his love? Of course not. The good news is that God loves us as we are, right now! The proof of this astonishingly good news is contained in the second statement about our king —

2. Jesus "*has freed us from our sins by his own blood.*"

That statement is good news, however, only if you believe you have some sins to be freed from. If you do not — if you are basically satisfied with your life as it is — then *that* is your good news: your good moral character. Congratulations! Jesus Christ has good news *only* for people of bad moral character — people who realize that their lives are a tangle of loose ends, of broken resolutions, of high ideals and mediocre performance. The Gospel is good news only for those who can say with the apostle Paul: "The good which I want to do, I fail to do; but what I do is the wrong which is against my will" (Romans 7:19).

This good news begins with the statement that Jesus our king loves us. He does not love some idealized version of us, the people we would like to be and keep on hoping we will be one day. No. Jesus loves us as we are right now. He loved us enough to die for us.

Jesus' voluntary death on our behalf in some mysterious but real way makes up for our innumerable shortcomings and sins and failures. Our vicious circle of high resolutions and mediocre performance has been broken by a power, and a love, greater than our own: the power and love of Jesus our king, "the firstborn from the dead and ruler of the kings of earth," as our second reading calls him. Unlike all other kings, he rules by love, not by power, serving his subjects rather than lording it over them. That is Gospel. That is good news.

Yet there is more.

238

3. *Jesus "has made us a royal nation of priests in the service of his God and Father."*

That sentence from our second reading means that through baptism, we share in both the priesthood and kingship of Jesus our king. We exercise our *priesthood* when we gather here, as God's people, to "do this" with the bread and wine, as our king and high priest commanded the night before he died. We obey that command *collectively*. The human priest is necessary to lead us in this greatest act of the Church's worship. But we all present our sacrificial offering and worship together with the priest, who is only the human representative of the one true priest, Jesus Christ. He is the principal celebrant of every Mass.

In baptism Jesus also gave us a share in his kingship by making us members, the second reading says, of "a royal nation." We exercise our *kingship* as Jesus does: by serving people. A religion that is limited to obtaining blessings for ourselves, with few consequences in daily life, is not the religion of Jesus Christ. Like him, we are called to serve others in everyday life: at home, at work, wherever we encounter people, and whether we find them lovable or not. That alone fulfills the commission given to us when, in baptism, Jesus our king made us citizens and members of his "royal nation of priests in the service of his God and Father."

We who in baptism have been made members of that "royal nation of priests" are called to live amid the darkness of our world in the light of the vision proclaimed in the closing words of our second reading:

See, he comes amid the clouds! Every eye shall see him, even of those who pierced him. All the people of the earth shall lament him bitterly. So it is to be! Amen!

239

Repeatedly the Bible says that Jesus our king *is* coming. That we have not witnessed his return after twenty centuries does not prove the Bible wrong. This is still "the last age," even if its termination is delayed according to our limited human reckoning.

How often we hear people say: "We don't know what is coming." Perhaps we have said that ourselves. It is true. We do *not* know what is coming. But we do know *who* is coming! Our second reading tells us who he is:

The Alpha and the Omega, the One who is and who was and who is to come, the Almighty!

Immaculate Conception of the B.V.M. (Dec. 8)

Genesis 3:9-15, 20; Luke 1:26-38

"HAIL MARY, FULL OF GRACE."

● *To contrast the age-old dream of human independence with the figure of Mary, the example of total dependence.*

Ever since men and women have lived on this earth they have dreamed of becoming totally independent and self-sufficient. Which one of us has not longed at some time to say with the poet W.E. Henley (1849-1903):

I am the master of my fate:
I am the captain of my soul.

We find signs of this universal longing for independence everywhere: in the popular song, "I'll Do it My Way," in the comic book figure and movie hero Superman. Superman is totally self-sufficient. He can do anything he wants. He wins all his battles, overcomes all obstacles and every enemy. He is subject to no restrictions. The man of complete independence, Superman has, of course, no need of God.

Though man has dreamed of independence from the dawn of life, deep in his heart and soul he has always known that this dream is unattainable. The ancient Greeks enshrined this knowledge in a myth about a man who sought total independence: Prometheus, who stole fire from the gods and in punishment was chained to a rock where vultures tore at his vitals.

The ancient Hebrews had a story with the same theme. We heard it in our first reading. The characters in that story were

241

called Adam and Eve. In Hebrew those are not proper names, however. Adam is simply Hebrew for Man. Eve means Woman, the mother of all humankind. They too dreamed of independence. They decided to do it their way, not God's way. The story tells the consequences: shame and the loss of the happiness they had enjoyed as long as they lived in dependence on their Creator and in obedience to his laws. Which of us has not had that experience, in some form? It is the story not of two individuals, but of Everyman and Everywoman.

The Prometheus myth and the Genesis story of man's fall both tell us what, deep in our hearts, we know. We can never be totally self-sufficient and independent. Which one of us was able to choose our own parents, our brothers and sisters? Could any of us select our talents, our temperaments, our bodies, our minds? Which of us could map out in advance the course of our lives?

Every human life begins in total dependence. What could be more dependent than a baby in its mother's womb? How many millions of unborn infants today knock softly on life's door only to be refused admittance by mothers who fear, often under pressure from others, especially men, that the baby's birth could be inconvenient, an obstacle to the independence and self-sufficiency we constantly seek?

That any one of us is alive today is only because we were *accepted* by our parents — our mothers, especially — before we had established any claim to acceptance. We are alive, the theologians would say, because of *grace* — by a gratuitous act of acceptance and love that we had done nothing to deserve.

We can live happily only to the extent that we continue to feel accepted and loved by others. A life without that acceptance and love is a life of utter loneliness — hell on earth.

Mother Teresa calls loneliness "the greatest disease of our time."

One of the great *causes* of loneliness today is the idea that we get what we deserve and only what we deserve. If we want people to accept and love us, society tells us, we must first do something to *earn* this acceptance. What a terrible obstacle to human happiness that idea is! How many people in our world are lonely and otherwise miserable because they feel, at bottom, that they have not done enough, that they are not lovable?

Today's feast gives the lie to that cruel idea, so destructive of human happiness. Mary is the type and example of a person whose acceptance in love, not just by her mother but also and supremely by God, was totally gratuitous. The dogma we celebrate today is this: that Mary, from the first moment of her conception in the womb of her mother, by the special choice of God and in view of the merits of her Son, already foreseen by God, was protected by God from every taint of sin. What is *unique* in this is not the fact of Mary's protection from sin, but its timing. What happened to Mary at her conception happened to each of us at baptism.

What did Mary do to *earn* or *deserve* this privilege? Nothing! She was chosen by the free, gratuitous act of God. How did Mary *respond* to her choice, when she received what could only have been the first hint of what was to come? Today's Gospel tells us. She responded as any girl in the same situation would respond: with perplexity, fear, and confusion. She was "deeply troubled" by the words of God's messenger. She asked in perplexity: "How can this be since I do not know man?"

Most important of all, however, Mary responded to this perplexity and fearful announcement by *renouncing all claim to independence*: "I am the maidservant of the Lord. Let it be done to me as you say." Not then, nor ever, did Mary think for one moment of being the mistress of her fate or the captain of her soul. She knew herself to be totally dependent on God. She accepted this total dependence.

It is because of this acceptance that we, with all generations, call Mary blessed. That word "blessed" means "happy." Mary is the type of the supremely happy person because she renounced the age-old quest of humankind for self-sufficiency and independence. She is happy because she knows that everything she is and has is sheer gift, the result not of anything she achieved, but entirely of what she gratuitously received from God.

Can there be any doubt that Mary's example is the antidote we need so desperately today to the enormous amount of misery produced by our modern quest for happiness through achievement and independence? Mary tells us that we shall find happiness, fulfillment and peace to the extent, and only to the extent, that we renounce independence and, like her, acknowledge our total dependence on God. Because that is so difficult, we ask Mary's help as we join in the Church's ancient prayer, the common possession of peasants and popes, of scholars and simple believers alike:

Holy Mary, Mother of God,
Pray for us sinners now, and at the hour of our death. Amen.

Assumption of Mary (Aug. 15)

Luke 1:39-56

MARY, WOMAN OF FAITH.

* *To present Mary as a model of trusting faith.*

How much we Catholics used to hear about Mary! How little, by contrast, we seem to hear about her today. Does Marian devotion belong to a now-past era of Church history? Not at all. The Fathers of the Second Vatican Council, which met at Rome each fall from 1962 through 1965, considered Mary so central to our Catholic faith that they incorporated their teaching about her into the document which our present Holy Father called, the day after his election as pope on October 16, 1978, the "Magna Carta of the Council": the Constitution on the Church. There the Council says that Mary "shines forth on earth, until the day of the Lord shall come [see 2 Peter 3:10], a sign of sure hope and solace to the wandering people of God" (68).

That phrase, "the wandering people of God," recurs often in the Council's documents. It expresses the consciousness we have in the Church today of being *underway to a goal we have not yet reached.* Our journey is beset by difficulties and dangers. We are reminded of them every day: in the morning headlines, on the television news each evening. Precisely in such a time Mary is not less important to us, but more.

Mary's own pilgrimage was beset with difficulties and dangers. We know remarkably little about Mary's life. That little is enough, however, to show that she often had to walk in darkness. There were many things that, as Luke tells us, she "did not understand" (Luke 2:50).

What did Mary understand about the angel's message that even before her marriage to Joseph she was to become the mother of God's Son? She understood at least this: that in a tiny village where everyone knew everyone else and gossip was rife, she was to be an unmarried mother. Yet Mary responded without hesitation in trusting faith: "I am the maidservant of the Lord. Let it be done to me as you say" (Luke 1:38).

That act of faith was not blind. Young as Mary was (and the scripture scholars think she may have been only fifteen), she asked what any girl in her position would have asked: "How can this be since I do not know man?" (Luke 1:34) Even this question, however, reflects faith. Mary was questioning not so much God and his ways as her own ability to *understand* God's ways.

Nor was Mary's faith a once-for-all thing. It needed to be constantly renewed. Joseph wanted to break their engagement. In the Jerusalem temple Mary heard the aged Simeon prophesy her Son's rejection and his mother's suffering (Luke 2:34f). In time Mary's Son left home. Often thereafter he seemed to be fulfilling his own command about "hating" parents and other close relatives, and one's "own life too" (Luke 14:26).

At Cana, the site of his first miracle, Jesus appeared to treat his mother with perplexing disrespect (see John 2:4). Even at the Last Supper Jesus made no place for his mother. Only at Calvary was she permitted to stand beside her now-dying Son, along with "the disciple Jesus loved" (John 19:26). He was deliberately left anonymous, some scripture scholars believe, to represent the ideal follower of Jesus Christ in any age and any place.

There on Calvary Mary experienced the full truth of Simeon's prophecy of three decades before, that a sword would pierce her own soul. There she shared the anguish of her dying Son, as he cried: "My God, my God, why have you forsaken me?" (Matthew 27:46) Calvary was the final and greatest test of Mary's faith, the place where she had to renew once again, as she had done so often before during her pilgrimage, the declaration of trusting faith with which she had begun: "Let it be done to me according to your word."

The last glimpse of Mary which Scripture gives us is just before Pentecost. With the apostles and Jesus' other relatives, she is praying for the descent of the Holy Spirit (Acts 1:14). Thereafter Mary disappears. Her work of bringing Christ to the world, and renewing her faith in God amid darkness and trials that she could not understand, was taken over by the Church.

How Mary's life ended we do not know. Pope Pius XII, in defining the truth of Mary's assumption that we celebrate today, deliberately left this point vague. The pope's 1950 definition says simply:

> When the course of her earthly life had ended, she was taken up body and soul into the glory of heaven.

The "body" the pope refers to in that sentence is Mary's new resurrection body: the body with which Jesus rose from the dead: the heavenly and spiritual body which, St. Paul says, each one of us will receive in heaven (see 1 Corinthians 15:35-53).

Trusting in the powerful intercession of Mary, the woman of faith, we rejoice on her festival as we pray:

> Holy Mary, Mother of God, pray for us sinners, now and at the hour of our death. Amen.

All Saints' Day (Nov. 1)

Revelation 7:2-4, 9-14; 1 John 3:1-3; Matthew 5:1-12

"A HUGE CROWD WHICH NO ONE COULD COUNT..."

• *To instill hope through the example of the saints.*

Why is today's Feast of All Saints so universally beloved? High on any list of reasons is the ground it gives us ordinary Christians for *hope*. The fact that the Church very early felt the need to have a feast in honor of *all* the saints reflects the conviction that there are too many of them to be identified. Most of the saints, today's feast tells us, are known only to God. That in itself gives us great encouragement.

Our first reading emphasized the vast number of the saints through the symbolic use of the number twelve. The Book of Revelation, from which the reading is taken, is rich in symbolism. Twelve symbolizes fullness. There were twelve months in the year and twelve tribes in Israel. The author of Revelation tells us that in his vision of heaven he learned that the number of those who were "sealed," or saved, was "one hundred and forty-four thousand." This figure combines twelve, the number of fullness, with a thousand, the number of vastness. Taken together the two figures indicate that no one is excluded from salvation.

The verses immediately following were omitted from today's first reading. They mention each of the twelve tribes of Israel by name and say that in each case the number of those saved was twelve thousand. Again the numbers of fullness and vastness are combined to show that *all* members of the tribe are saved.

The concluding part of the vision, which we did hear, shows that salvation extends not only to all Israel, but to the whole of humanity. Immediately after recording the presence in heaven of all members of all twelve tribes of Israel, the writer sees "a huge crowd which no one could count from every nation, race, people, and tongue." In symbolic imagery he was recording the fulfillment of God's desire that "all people should find salvation and come to know the truth" (1 Timothy 2:4).

The language of this first reading, and of the whole Book of Revelation from which it is taken, is *poetic*. It is *suggestive*, not descriptive. Heaven cannot be described in human language any more than God can be described. God, and the unseen, spiritual world of God, the angels, and the saints, are far too big and glorious to be captured in any speech known to humankind.

That is the clear teaching of our second reading, where St. John writes: "What we shall be later has not yet come to light." All we know, John says, is that in heaven "we shall be like [God], for we shall see him as he is." Scripture nowhere gives us precise answers to questions about life beyond death, or about the present existence of the saints. Scripture tells us only what we need to know for life here and now.

An important part of this knowledge is Jesus' teaching in today's Gospel. The so-called Beatitudes which it contains were not addressed by Jesus to everyone indiscriminately, but only to those who were willing to follow him completely. For them, Jesus says, ordinary worldly standards and expectations are *reversed*. The poor are made rich; the sorrowful are comforted; the lowly are raised up; those who hunger for God's holiness are filled; the merciful experience mercy; the single-hearted see God; the peacemakers are God's children; and those who are persecuted for their faithfulness to God are vindicated and filled with joy.

The saints are all those for whom those beautiful promises have already been fulfilled. Today's feast gives us hope by reminding us that the vast majority of the saints are known only to God. With increased confidence, therefore, we can pray that Jesus' promises will be fulfilled for us too.

Today's feast gives us yet another reason for hope. It is this. The saints are not only far more *numerous* than we normally suppose. They are also much more *ordinary*.

The saints are just the sinners who kept on trying!

Subject Index